I Am More

Devan Millsong

First edition October, 2022

Manufactured in the United States of America

Scriptures referred to in this book are taken from the most up to date translations of the Holy Bible published by Zondervan Publishing House and provided online by biblegateway.com.

Published by Victory Vision Publishing and Consulting
www.victoryvision.org

Imprint RMDM Publications

Paperback ISBN: 979-8-9870081-0-2
eBook ISBN: 979-8-9870081-1-9

DEDICATION

To my daughters, with prayers that you never feel like less, my husband, with wishes I had met you sooner so I could've loved you longer, and my parents, for always loving me in spite of me.

And to…
Missa, my courage.
Penny, my vision.
My in-laws, my cheerleaders.
Sallie Rose, my guide.

But mostly to the survivors who bravely told their stories – and the ones who still have stories to tell.

This book is for you.

YOU. ARE. MORE.

CONTENTS

Chapter One

Soul Worth Sharing

———————————

I am more than what happened to me.

I AM more.

I.

Am.

MORE.

I am MORE.

Yes, I AM.

Sometimes, that last sentence still has to be said. There are wounded moments that, even now, after all these years, feel emotionally gaping and raw when I need a reminder that what happened *to* me does not *define* me.

There are times I struggle to believe I am more than the sexual assault that sneers demoralizingly now and then from the back of my brain. Countless shields of life's joy usually confine it to my mind's far shadows, and I'm thankful to no longer struggle hour to hour or minute to minute. There is no shame or humiliation in what happened. So, if there are days when that menacing memory rears its ugly head, I'll live with it. Those days are passing thoughts, lingering memories, fleeting moments, with zero real control.

I am more than what was done to me.

I am more than how I was treated.

I am more than what was said to me and about me.

I am more than what I thought about myself.

I am more than how I acted in the days, weeks, months, and years since then.

I am more than what happened.

I. *Am*. More.

Most of the time I believe it, and I have finally allowed myself to be okay with not believing it *all* the time. It's in those occasional moments when I'm not okay that I give myself permission to feel anger toward the people who hurt me. While many peoples' first reactions after an assault are to be furious at the people who hurt them, my reaction was to wonder what I did wrong and what I could have done differently, to carry the burden of blame on my own shoulders, and to be certain that the things in my life that went wrong were solely the products of my own choices.

After operating with that perspective for long enough, it was difficult to channel my anger in any direction other than down a self-destructive path. Rather than turning to prayer and guidance from Above, seeking counseling from a trained professional, and allowing myself time to heal as a whole person – body, mind, and soul – I assessed my part in the problem and kept chanting, "I *can't* control *others*. I *can* control *my* reactions."

Get a grip, Devan[1].
Are you going to let anger and hurt feelings
rule you from now on?
Are you going to let this awful thing control your heart
and ruin relationships?
Of course not, so soldier on, girl, and let's go.
Put it behind you.
Not every guy is like that,

SO GET OVER IT.

I tried to tell myself this was a strong outlook for moving past sexual assault and understanding that not every person in life was destined to hurt me, but it wasn't exactly the best approach for my mental, emotional, or spiritual health without first having actually dealt with what happened and given myself time to accept it. I'm the queen of compartmentalizing – pain of all kinds, physical, mental, emotional. They all have their own fancily decorated boxes in various parts of beautifully-functioning-while-damaged me.

---

[1] All names in *I Am More* have been changed, including my own, to protect each person who has moved on to a different place in life.

Store them in a dark corner.

Life goes on.

No time to stop.

If you stop, it catches you.

And "it" can be lots of things on any given day if you have ignored enough things for too long.

Some days, though, I give in and resent freely with every fiber of loathing and bitterness I can summon from the immeasurable depths tunneled out by years of compartmentalizing. I know I am more than what happened, and I know the people who hurt me have no bearing on my life now; but there are days a sound, a smell, a thought, a dream, some small glimpse of the way a hair falls around a face – *any completely random thing* – can set my brain to whirling and thinking in uncontrollable ways, and thinking leads to compartmentalizing and rationalizing. These days, I usually step away from the fancily decorated and damaged boxes in my brain (or at least I try to) and allow myself a few moments to break down and to be okay with not being okay.

As broken as it feels, it's healthy. In those moments, I pray. I ask God to grant my aching brain peace, to allow me to feel things, to remind me to breathe, to love, to forgive. It's an ongoing, uneasy process, and sometimes the person who needs forgiving is simply me. Most days, life feels like calm, peaceful waters, but on days when life's oceans get a little choppy, quiet moments of prayer, a good set of earphones, and my favorite playlist usually smooth out the rough, nauseating waves. Writing this book certainly helped but also opened my eyes to many things.

In fact, writing this book has been the hardest thing I've ever had to do.

Simply wrenching out that last sentence was a labor-intensive, take-a-deep-breath-or-twenty, Jesus-take-the-wheel process. I lost count of how many times I backspaced struggling to decide between "one of the hardest things" and "*the* hardest thing" when, in reality, there was no choice to make. There was one true answer, and the more I toyed with it, the idea of hedging the wording became outright offensive. I overthought to the point of absurdity even though it really wouldn't make a difference to anyone other than me.

But it does make a substantial difference *to me*.

Every word of this book has made a difference – a painfully gut-wrenching, like-pulling-teeth-to-get-it-out, why-am-I-doing-this, worth-it-all difference. This book began with a mission to write about a single incident that occurred with one person and share my story of sexual assault.

Plain and simple. Tell my story.

But no.

Life is rarely that simple.

Writing this book is, was, and hopefully will remain the hardest thing I have ever done. I didn't think it would be. I didn't set out to agonize over it. It was my chance to finally, after years of avoiding the subject, tell my story of being sexually assaulted and give a voice to others who needed their voices to be heard somewhere other than their own hearts and memories.

Writing about it wasn't supposed to be the difficult part. Living through it was difficult enough. Avoiding the topic for so many years was a frustratingly difficult game of isolation. Deciding it was time to give up that game was difficult. Once the decision had been made, though, there wasn't supposed to be anything difficult about the writing. I expected that to flow easily, like sitting down to write a blog or a social media post.

I'll tell my story, and I'll tell other people's stories,
just as I've known all these years I was supposed to do.
No problem. I'm a writer.
I've been writing since I was old enough to hold a pencil.
I've got this.
I'll start with my own story to lay the foundation.
What could be so difficult about that?

What could be so difficult indeed…

Start with realizing I had to tell a great deal more than what happened during my assault to fully explain what needed to be said and that the assault was merely a small part of my story. Follow that with a series of painful epiphanies about why the 18 years of my life between the assault and starting the book played out the way they did based on choices that pre-date the assault and that were only made worse by what happened.

Add to that the revelation that there were people with similar experiences who I never realized shared this pain regardless of how long or how well I'd known them. There were stories that needed and deserved to be told. My story was a story I'd known for many years was mine to tell, even though I'd tried to avoid it. Throughout the years, every time I thought I'd moved on and successfully buried the assault in the past, it came right back. That's what happens when you fool yourself into thinking you're okay when you aren't.

Sometimes, no matter how much time passes and no matter how much you think you're okay with something that happened to you, it unexpectedly parks on your chest like a bear. A bear who swallowed a lead pipe filled with concrete. A bear bound in 100 yards of razor blades and barbed wire dipped in a blistering cocktail of rubbing alcohol and hot sauce. Mr. Bear also brought along his favorite blanket stitched with the threads of panic attack, shame, and embarrassment and quickly settled in quite uncomfortably.

This burdensome boy and his souvenirs of pain are hibernating on your chest as you fight to squash the memories, sometimes simply struggling to breathe and to keep smiling as if nothing is wrong, something you're rather accustomed to already anyway, but this time?

Well, this time is different. This time feels as if you might not come up for air and that smile you hide behind might just break your face.

If you've experienced that feeling, you know what I mean. You may even think, "Bear? Yeah, right! More like an elephant." Whatever image that painfully unfortunate moment conjures, the feeling is fairly universal – time-stopping, breath-snatching, heart-crushing, tear-inducing, head-spinning, all-out-soul-consuming pain.

For a sexual assault survivor, the memories can resurface minutes, days, months, or years later. You may live through prolonged periods of acceptance, personal strength, and empowerment.

Life is okay.

Life is good.

You're okay.

You're good.

The person who hurt you is irrelevant. You refuse to allow that person to have a single moment's power over any part of your body, mind, heart, or soul. There you are rocking along through your day, and *BAM*.

Life happens.

Mr. Bear takes up residence on your chest, and the seemingly tangible memory of what happened is so heavy your lungs fight for a single second of air. Trying to shove the feeling away is like battling that tangled mess of razor blades and barbed wire.

You didn't know to be on the lookout. You couldn't have. A reminder, however small it might be – there it is. Something you didn't see coming, just as you never could have predicted what was going to happen to you, that thing that started it all, that incident that altered your life's path perhaps in some minor way or perhaps in immeasurably excruciating, enduring ways from which you have not recovered and often wonder if you ever will.

> *Hello, memories.*
> *Yes, let's float around in this pool*
> *of rubbing alcohol and hot sauce*
> *and let our wounds sting for a while.*
> *No, I don't need to breathe.*
> *Breathing leads to living and thinking*
> *and a beating, feeling,*
> *blood-pumping, body-moving heart,*
> *and the last thing I need right now*
> *is to move from this spot.*

But you do move. You have to.

Life doesn't shut down just because you do. So, you hug Mr. Bear and let him hibernate to keep him quiet. You move on about your day hoping no one sees you struggling under the weight of something so piercing.

Maybe it's just me. Maybe I'm the only mental case who, after being assaulted, strapped on my issues like a bulletproof vest and soldiered through a muddled life with a counterfeit smile. For 18 years, I ran. I set it aside. I maintained an "it was what it was" out-look never once admitting I was a victim. I felt guilt and shame and embarrassment and regret beyond any possibility of measurement, but the word "victim" never crossed into my vocabulary.

Off and on through the years, I heard a small voice in my sub-conscious whispering, "There are so many others like you. Tell your story so they can tell theirs. *Go tell their stories.*"

I ignored it.

That's not my story to tell, I thought.

As a writer by trade, I thought I might someday write a book, but it certainly wouldn't be about *that*. Still, though, despite my insistence that I wasn't a victim, now and then, I heard those commanding words in the back of my mind.

At those moments, I was inevitably reminded of a song from my favorite movie, *The Color Purple*. In an iconic scene, the Shug Avery character is singing one Sunday morning at the juke joint with the other "sinners." She catches a drift of faint notes across the field as the choir sings "Maybe God Is Trying to Tell You Something" up the road at the small country church her father pastors.

Shug has suffered the heartbreak of wanting to restore her long-broken relationship with her father, and at that moment, something ignites in her soul. She takes off up the dirt road with a parade of juke joint sinners in tow, bursts through the church doors, and leads the entire congregation in one of the most stirring renditions of "Maybe God Is Trying to Tell You Something" the world could ever hope to witness.

At one point, she stops singing, hesitates at the altar, and slowly steps forward to embrace her father. While the sounds of holy praises keep rocking along, she says in his ear, "See, Daddy? Sinners have soul, too." There is a brief, painful delay, but he finally stretches his arms wide, ever so hesitatingly, to place them around his estranged daughter, and if you can keep a dry eye, you're certainly a stronger person than I am. Shug and her father stand in front of the congregation hugging and smiling, and for the first time in years, their fractured world seems healed.

Will they keep talking? At that moment, it doesn't matter. God tried to tell them something for a long time, and they finally listened.

That's how I felt for so long until I stopped running and started writing. When I finally sat down to begin writing after all those years and embraced my God-given task, it felt every bit as satisfying and healing as seeing Shug finally hug her father. Through all those years I thought that nagging feeling I kept getting was my conscience whispering for me to tell someone what happened, so I ignored it.

But if you know anything about how God works,
He doesn't just tell you what He wants
you to do and leave it at that.
He keeps working on you until you listen.

Looking back, I truly believe that persistent feeling was God's insisting that my love of writing was given to me as a gift for this purpose – to tell the stories of sexual assault survivors at a time in history when their voices would finally not just be heard but *understood*.

I heard "Maybe God Is Trying to Tell You Something" in my head for years. I heard it in my heart. Sometimes I felt as if I heard that song all the way to the core of who I was and was sure people could hear it playing like a soundtrack all around me as I trudged through my days. No matter how much I ignored it, the familiar tune kept right on playing. Over and over and over, I felt as if I heard in the background while the notes played, "This is what I've told you to do, and until you do what I've asked, you're not going to successfully write anything else. *This* is your assignment."

And that's essentially how it was – each time I tried to write other things, I was met with dead ends and writer's block, yet I still refused to tell my story. I didn't feel as if I had anything worth telling. By my overly rationalized thinking, I wasn't a victim, so there was no story to tell. It was something that happened to a girl who put herself in a position she shouldn't have been in.

What happened was **my fault**. *End of story.*

Sometimes I tried not to think about that night at all, but then something would unexpectedly come along to make me think of him, of what happened. That's always been the case. I suppose it always will be. That's sort of the nature of things like sexual assault. No matter how much time passes and how much you think you've dealt with it and moved on, it's always going to be there. It happened. You can't take back that day, that moment, that situation you were in that brought that person into your life.

One day not long after ignoring that song and those words in my head once again telling me to "go tell their stories," I had a moment that brought me back to the assault in such a powerful way that I had to walk away from the computer before I could finish reading an article that dropped into my social media newsfeed like a lead balloon.

There was a picture of a clean-cut college student next to an article detailing his arrest for assaulting a young woman after they had been drinking together at a party. As I read, I was shocked to realize the author spent more time blaming the victim's drinking and pointing out the alleged perpetrator's athletic record than anything else.

What world have I slipped into where this is okay?
Am I living some sort of nightmare
where this is good journalism or decent judgment?

As I scrolled through other articles about the incident, the same references repeated in each one. They pointed out his swim team accomplishments and what a promising Olympic career he had ahead of him. I had never heard of Brock Allen Turner before this incident, but he sure seemed to be highly respected for someone accused of such appalling things.

The judge in the case evidently thought Turner was a decent guy despite the graphic testimony and subsequent conviction because he was letting him off on the charges with what felt to me like barely a slap on the wrist compared to the severity of the crime. A few months in jail for a crime that this young woman would suffer mental and emotional damage from for the rest of her life? I read the article thinking this must surely be a twisted joke.

Numerous articles were posted online over the following days, weeks, and months, and I became nearly obsessed with the absolute disgust I felt seeing Turner's smiling face on the screen. Every time I clicked on an article, I hoped to read that this young lady might receive justice for what happened to her, but every time, I became more disheartened.

According to the articles, the two men who happened upon the scene stopped Turner as he penetrated the victim with a foreign object while she lay unconscious on the ground by a dumpster, mostly naked and unable to consent to anything that was happening. The victim wrote a statement, which she read in open court, and it was one of the most impactful things I've ever encountered, especially in one particular section where she described how she was found:

> "One day, I was at work, scrolling through the news on my phone, and came across an article. In it, I read and learned for the first time about how I was found unconscious, with my hair disheveled, long necklace wrapped around my neck, bra pulled out of my dress, dress pulled off over my shoulders and pulled up above my waist, that I was butt naked all the way down to my boots, legs spread apart, and had been penetrated by a foreign object by someone I did not recognize. This was how I learned what happened to me, sitting at my desk reading the news at work. I learned what happened to me the same time everyone else in the world learned what happened to me. That's when the pine needles in my hair made sense, they didn't fall from a tree. He had taken off my underwear, his fingers had been inside of me. I don't even know this

person. I still don't know this person. When I read about me like this, I said, this can't be me. This can't be me. I could not digest or accept any of this information. I could not imagine my family having to read about this online. I kept reading. In the next paragraph, I read something that I will never forgive; I read that according to him, I liked it. I liked it. Again, I do not have words for these feelings. At the bottom of the article, after I learned about the graphic details of my own sexual assault, the article listed his swimming times. *'She was found breathing, unresponsive with her underwear six inches away from her bare stomach curled in fetal position. By the way, he's really good at swimming.'* Throw in my mile time if that's what we're doing. I'm good at cooking, put that in there, I think the end is where you list your extra-curriculars to cancel out all the sickening things that've happened."[2]

As I read her statement and realized the details of what happened to this young lady who had no opportunity to say "No" or to fight back and whose entire life was altered by one night, I started thinking of the endless ways she had been so blatantly discounted in the media and the judicial process and began thinking of my own assault. Her experience was nothing short of horrifying. My story didn't seem nearly as traumatic, but after reading what she suffered and how she faced Turner in court, my own assault rolled through my mind like a perpetual highlight reel.

---

[2] County of Santa Clara, California, court documents, posted online at: https://www.sccgov.org/sites/da/newsroom/newsreleases/Documents/B-Turner%20VIS.pdf

The familiar opening notes of "Maybe God is Trying to Tell You Something" queued up, and the chorus soon rumbled on repeat. It didn't just play in my mind anymore, though. It followed me in daily life. I heard it on television, people mentioned it in conversations, friends referenced it in texts.

Randomly. For no reason. There it was.

I didn't listen. I almost never do.

I was as determined as ever that it would never be my story to tell. As long as things affected only me, I didn't worry over them. My assault wasn't anyone else's problem.

Case closed. No need for discussion.

However, if you ignore God's song when the volume is low, He eventually turns it up, and that's just what He did about a month after the Turner case began to die down. A long-time friend texted me to confide that she had been taken advantage of by her former fiancé while she was intoxicated. She trusted him to watch over her in a moment of weakness but instead found herself waking up a victim.

Cue the familiar music and images of Shug's marching toward that small country church with the whole juke joint in tow.

Okay, Big Guy.

I'm listening, and You're clearly talking directly to me.

Now, it affects someone I love.

I'll go tell their stories.

I spent quite a bit of time listening to my friend Ashley talk about her assault and sharing with her how I was impacted by my own. She's one strong lady. I was honored she opened her heart to me and allowed me to include her story here. We've been friends for many years, but after an assault, knowing where to turn can be impossible. Looking back, I feel certain our paths were somehow predestined to cross for this purpose.

As the unfortunately Divine inspiration for this book, Ashley was the first person I interviewed. Without her, I never would have gotten the courage to stop running from my story and face nearly two decades of denying I was a victim. Because of her, I was able to finally admit to someone other than my husband (who up to that point was the only person who knew), "I was sexually assaulted."

It still isn't easy.

Through this writing process, I've had the opportunity to share my story countless times, but I still hesitate to use the term "rape." The first time I said it, I nearly threw up. Tiny, stinging tears welled in my eyes. My lungs felt as if they collapsed. I took several seconds to catch my breath and give my world permission to spin again. I actively fought the urge to apologize to the friend to whom I was confiding.

To this minute, I have no idea why I felt that way. I had just begun writing and felt a profound obligation to reveal the entire story in all its long-kept secretiveness to one of my oldest and dearest friends – the only person who knows both me and the man who assaulted me. I was thinking of my attacker quite a bit as I wrote and needed to say his full name out loud to someone who knew him.

Once it had been said, his name surrounded me.

Each of its letters split into thousands of carving knives, flinging chunks of me wildly in every direction like a novice butcher hacking a slab of meat. I was suffocating amidst this mental barrage of pain simply from uttering a single five-letter word – "raped." Barely able to move, I was cemented in a mix of fear that his name would become something more, something tangible, something real, something I had to feel, touch, smell again. I had put so much behind me in the 18 years since it had happened, and talking about it openly was a far different experience than allowing it to simmer quietly in the back of my memories.

I realized as my friend and I talked that I'd been holding my breath while pondering this ridiculously vivid knife scenario as she shrieked into the phone, "He did *what*?!" Gasping for air, I returned to breathing suddenly, deeply, pushing away that awful word.

> *Take it back!*
> *Why did you say that?*
> *Tell her you lied.*
> *Tell her it's a sick joke.*

She wouldn't have believed me. She knows me well enough to know I would never make up something like that, and from what I learned through the course of our conversation, she didn't question whether he could be capable of such a thing. We talked for nearly an hour, and the end of our conversation took with it a burden I'd carried for far too long.

I needed to say his name out loud. I needed, in some strange way, to claim it, to own what happened. It was an odd coming-out of sorts, and as the only person who knows both of us, my friend was the logical choice to "come out" to.

Telling my family was perhaps the most difficult part of the writing process, and I procrastinated until the entire book was nearly finished. After so many years had passed since the assault, it was a particularly challenging subject to bring up.

How could I tell them why I didn't want to say anything
back then about such a life-altering event?
How could I explain my need to reveal
all the personal things I discussed?
How could I share this personal incident that felt like
a dirty little secret because I hid it for so long?

It took me what felt like a lifetime of forevers to broach the subject with my family for fear of how this inconvenient truth would damage our relationship; however, what was an inconvenient truth for them was my long-time norm. I understood that the things which needed to be shared would be tough to hear; but my family had to know before the world got to flip the pages of my life and see these events and decisions that had stitched together the tattered boundaries of my path for nearly two decades before I finally faced them.

For some, it was a long-awaited aha moment about why I had made certain choices and a chance to hug it out and offer sympathy.

For others, it was a feet-soaked-in-alcohol stroll across broken glass down Inconvenient Truth Lane.

Regardless of which option ultimately proved to be true for each person, there were still things that needed to be said. They were difficult, but they were said, and we all survived. Some more easily than others, but we all survived. I still feel as if there are a few people in my life who permanently moved their residence to Inconvenient Truth Lane, but I can't fix that for them. I can only accept that I finally moved out of that address myself and hope they someday join me.

To understand what led up to my experience with this man, though, I have realized it's important to understand the person I was when it took place and what led me to him, who I was before him, and who I was after him. I was not the same person after my experience with him, and I changed in ways I didn't realize until I began writing and thinking back on my life.

Talking to sexual assault survivors about their stories has also helped me define a path of healing and reconciliation, and I've more accurately defined the twists and turns my path has taken since then and even before it happened – the things that, ultimately, were what led me to that place and time.

It's also important to share that this isn't the only incident of this kind that has occurred in my life. I wish I could say it is, but it unfortunately isn't. There were more than a fair share of cruel people who made their way through my life, some of whom I invited in knowing they didn't need to be there and some who forced their way in, but there is a particular event that shaped me as a person and was a defining factor in much of my life after it happened.

I just had to quit running from it long enough to address it head-on and let God try to tell me something.

Well, I finally listened, and this sinner discovered she had some soul worth sharing. Once I let that wall down, the choir sure was singing a beautiful song. Unlike Shug's father who took a minute to stretch his arms out and bring his daughter back into his life, God didn't hesitate one bit when He wrapped His arms around me and covered me in His grace and love. I'm thankful to be in that place of peace on a daily basis now.

Writing my story has been difficult, and it doesn't get much easier the more times I share it. As you read the stories in the later chapters of survivors who share how they overcame what took place in their lives, keep in mind that this book is not intended to be an easy read. Our stories may be graphic at times, but they are not sensationalized to create a more interesting book.

They are real.

We are real.

We are people who experienced altering events. This is life. This is what survivors have lived. And we continue to live it because we get to relive it, sometimes every day over and over *and over* in our minds and hearts. Sometimes it feels as if we can feel it and taste it and smell it.

I hear it a lot.

Barely a day passes that I don't hear the words my attacker said to me that night pinging from one side of my head to the other. First, I hear it in one ear. Then, I hear it in the other ear. I can still hear his voice, the exact tone he used, where he placed the emphasis on each word, the slightly whispered harshness with which he said them, the way he was slightly out of breath...

You don't forget. It's real. It's our lives. The victims. The survivors. The sinners with soul like Shug singing with that choir and letting our stories be heard as God has instructed us to do. We're found here on these pages, but we aren't alone. There are so many women – and plenty of men – who live every day with stories of their own to share.

And we are more than what happened to us.

Chapter Two

The Road to Less

Sharing my story means going back. Who was I before that moment? Growing up, I was the type of girl my friends would've probably voted "Least Likely to Ever Be a Victim of Anything Because She's Too Naive and Boring To Do Anything."

I definitely wasn't the girl who was going to come out of a still-mostly-drunk fog in a room she had never been in before that moment with a guy on top of her demanding that she say his name. But we'll get to that. Who I was before that night is important in order to understand what brought me to that room and to that place in my life.

Growing up, I wasn't perfect, of course, but I was probably better than most at staying out of trouble and being a decent enough kid – straight A's, at the church every time the doors were open from around age 13 until I graduated from high school, in just about every club picture in the yearbook, editor of the high school newspaper. I was a rule-following Daddy's girl who was as strait-laced and scared of my own shadow as the day was long.

To say I was naïve doesn't begin to describe me. I grew up before social media and information-on-the-go. If we wanted to know about our bodies or sexuality, we had to hope our parents were knowledgeable and bold enough to tell us or brave it up to the public library under the watchful eye of the crotchety librarian who knew exactly what we were doing as we giggled our way through the dusty, outdated encyclopedias.

I was a blank slate when it came to understanding my body and sex, so when I met Luke in the fall of my senior year of high school, my world was instantly upside down. I had turned 17 a week earlier, and Daddy knew right away that this 24-year-old, blue-eyed, fast-moving cowboy with a ladies'-man reputation around our small town was most definitely not the right person for young, sheltered me.

Of course, I knew better.

I was a painfully naïve 17, even by 1991's standards. As Daddy put it, I was "jailbait to that boy." Never mind that I was legally old enough to consent to a relationship with this man. In Daddy's eyes, that didn't matter. As he saw it, no man in his mid-20's had reason to be interested in a 17-year-old girl unless he had one thing on his mind, and, according to Daddy, he needed to find someone his own age to do *that* with.

Well, isn't that just like handing a stubborn,
inexperienced, teenage girl an invitation to fight?

Being with Luke meant standing up to my parents and going against their wishes for the first time. Every love story and movie I'd ever seen, heard of, or daydreamed about was playing through my head at that moment, and for a hormonal teenage girl, that's essentially what every drama-riddled second of my life had been building to. I swear I felt like Molly Ringwald in any John Hughes movie with an emotionally intense soundtrack swelling behind me as I starry-eyed strolled hand-in-hand with my angst through the halls of my school with books in front of me and a pouty face pondering how I would ever solve the dilemma of what to do about my awesomely perfect, charming guy and my heartbreakingly closedminded, strict parents.

Looking back, I nearly gag on my own irrationality, but to a teenage girl, the drama of it was significant and tangible and profound. It consumed every thought bouncing through my scattered brain. This man who had moved into our tiny town from a metropolitan area several states away was the light who appeared out of nowhere and made me feel I was something more than the overlooked girl I had always been.

Luke said things no one had ever said to me, looked at me with those bottomless blue eyes in ways no one had ever looked at me, and wanted to know me and touch me in ways no one had ever bothered to be interested. There were only hormonally challenged, goofy teenage boys at my school, and they mostly ignored me. If they talked to me, it was undoubtedly for one of two reasons – we were church friends or they needed an answer to a test question.

Luke was the first person who made my heart skip a beat in a way that went beyond adolescent boyfriend/girlfriend playfulness.

When he held my hand, I felt something *more*, something deeper, something connected, as if I could hold on forever, as if when he was gone, I wasn't breathing, and when he was there, everything made sense again.

Seventeen-year-old girls are drama queens – what can I say? *Especially me.*

I was so sheltered and unsure of myself. I grew up in a home where I idolized what my parents said and mostly took their discipline and rules to be the world's one-and-only way. Luke was the first person who made me contemplate the idea that I actually had a voice and opinions of my own, even though I didn't realize at the time how powerless I was to tell him "No."

Any time he asked something of me or told me we had plans, regardless of whether I agreed, I went along with it. So, when he wanted to have sex for the first time a couple of months after we met, even though I was reluctant, I agreed. In our small town, it was a rare thing for two people in a relationship to have waited as long as we did, especially a naïve, just-turned-17-year-old and a smooth-talking, aggressive 24-year-old.

He asked me to marry him a week after we met, and in my addled teen brain, saying "Yes" seemed like the fight-the-power, stick-it-to-my-parents, swept-up-in-emotion, what-a-great-story-this-is, I-finally-have-my-Molly-Ringwald-moment thing to do. Even with the giddy sense of power my secret gave me and a tiny chip of an engagement ring stashed deep in my purse, I remained hesitant to take the next step, mostly because I really didn't know what the next step required. Even knowing the power he had over me, he didn't try to persuade me physically. He seemed truly sympathetic about my reluctance, much more than the guys I grew up with would have been, and especially for someone with a great deal more experience than his new partner.

> *It does seem like the next logical step in our relationship,*
> *and I know he loves me.*
> *He's putting up with so much to be with me,*
> *and most guys would've broken up with me a long time ago*
> *if they had to go through so much secrecy just to see me.*

He was far more patient than he had to be. He could have been with other girls in town but chose to dedicate his time to me. Because of my sheltered life, the things to which he introduced me were more than I had imagined sex and relationships to be. When I say I was sheltered, I mean sheltered in its purest definition. As I mentioned earlier, these were the days before widespread Internet access and smartphones in every hand – there was no such thing as knowledge gratification at your fingertips. If you couldn't find what you wanted to know at the aforementioned ancient, outdated library, you found out from your friends or hoped your parents told you, and my parents weren't of a generation that liked to talk about that sort of thing.

Even the basic mechanics of the sexual experience escaped me. At some point I had learned guys have a thing called a penis but still didn't know what it looked like, and I knew about menstruation and that I had a uterus and a vagina. Somehow, these parts worked together without clothes between them, and, if you weren't careful, you could make a baby, although I wasn't clear the exact science of how that occurred.

That was about the limit of it. Sex bad. Abstinence good. The end.

Seriously.

That was where the knowledge ended. Luke never made fun of me about it, though, even when he realized I didn't know things had to be moved around or helped along or that there was a process to the whole thing. I didn't know people did anything with other parts of their bodies or what foreplay was other than kissing.

Once we started sleeping together, it was all we ever did. Every time we were able to sneak time together, we had sex. It became an expectation, one I didn't really mind and one I presumed was common among couples since I lacked any other perspective. Hollywood and pop culture in general raised me to believe that, as a woman, my worth and merit in a relationship were tied to how much my partner wanted to be with me in that way, and Luke was clearly interested in every inch of me.

When those fantastically blue eyes gazed into mine, it didn't matter that my parents had spent 17 years handcrafting me into an intelligent, independent young lady who should have known her value in life was not tied to such things and who should have had a strong enough mind to never blindly allow herself to be bossed around. When he looked at me, common sense ceased to exist. All that mattered was doing what I could to maintain our relationship, which – in my mind, at least – was the best thing that would ever happen to me.

When I left for college the following June, he expected me to be in my dorm room by a certain hour so he could call. If I had to be somewhere or didn't make it to the room in time, he wanted to know why, with whom I had spent my time and what we had done, why I was making up stories to try to cover where I really was, if there were guys where I had been, and why I had to go to college in the first place. The questions were endless. Sometimes, he was angry and defensive. Sometimes, he was sad I had left him behind.

We talked for a long time each night. Most nights, the calls were warm and caring and full of talk about people I met, interesting professors, things I learned, what he did at work, and my nightly reassurance that I planned to stay in for the night after we hung up. He said he was worried about my being out on campus alone at night and wasn't trying to control me – it was only for my "protection" because he couldn't be there to watch over me.

When he hung up, though, back in my hometown where he still lived, he was going out with friends to "just hang out," as he told me. Being in his mid-20's, there was nothing to stop him from doing whatever he wanted. At first, I didn't realize that there was also nothing to stop me from doing the things I wanted to do, but after a while, I began to find new friends and occasionally left the dorm after our calls. As much as I loved him, I wanted to experience college life and explore the world around me.

I didn't go looking for another man, but the stress in our relationship, the frequent arguments, and the growing suspicion that I was not the only girl in his life wore me down. After a few months at school, I met John, a nice guy who worked in the computer lab where I worked on assignments.

He was nice. He didn't tell me what to do. He wanted to know me, not touch me. He was smart with an intelligent humor, and he laughed a lot. He made me laugh, too. I didn't realize how long it had been since I had genuinely laughed or felt a flutter when someone talked to me or how long it had been since I had honestly wanted to be talked to.

We flirted and talked and spent a few nights walking around campus after he got off work at 10 p.m., well after my call with Luke. I justified my time with him by telling myself that I wasn't cheating. We weren't doing anything but talking and strolling around campus. We didn't even hold hands. The closest we came to even touching was one night when we were sitting on the steps of a campus building laughing about a story he told. I leaned across to the right as I laughed and casually lingered on his shoulder. It was a nice, comfortable moment shared between two people getting to know each other, but that was as far as it went. The only reason it sticks out after all these years is the deeply comfortable, awkward sigh we both let out before I leaned back the other way, as if we both wanted me to linger in the moment a little longer and both felt a little surprisingly happy in that time and space.

The next night, John called to ask if I wanted to go out to eat. *A real date*. Before I knew what was happening, I was headed out the door acting as if I weren't engaged to someone else. That "someone else" hadn't bothered to call the night before and hadn't been home late that night when I called, so I was reluctant to care much about what he thought. In my immaturity, going out seemed to be an adequate response.

John was a gentleman. He opened doors for me, both in the truck and at the restaurant. He asked what I wanted to eat and ordered for both of us but not until he asked my permission to do so. He made conversation like any other time we had spent time together but began talking more about his family and career plans. When he dropped me off at my dorm later, he left me with a kiss on the cheek. I saw the sweetest blush sweep across his olive complexion as he strolled back to his truck with a smile that equaled the one on my face.

We continued talking and hanging out for a couple of weeks. Talking to Luke became increasingly difficult, and I found myself standing up to him more each time we spoke. Meeting John had given me courage to draw a few lines in the sand with Luke, but I still couldn't get past the fear of antagonizing him and causing him to break up with me.

One night, as John pulled up at the university stadium where we were going walking, it began to rain, and it was soon an all-out thunderstorm. We sat in the truck talking, waiting for the storm to pass, inching closer and closer until we were next to each other. In the middle of talking, we started kissing. A little kissing led to a lot of kissing, and pretty soon, we were laid out in the truck all over each other with the rain hammering the truck window and every dramatic make-out scene from teen movies playing frame by frame in my mind.

When he started to take my shirt off, I sat up.

"I can't do this."

He stared back at me.

"Okay," he said. "I wasn't going to try to sleep with you. We're just fooling around."

Suddenly, my hidden Luke truths poured out, rapid-fire beating us like the rain on the windshield. I explained we had been together for a long time, that we were in a very tenuous place and had been for quite a while, and that it wasn't fair to either of them to be doing what we were doing. I told him I needed to end things once and for all with Luke before I could move on and that it wasn't right to be kissing him when I knew there was someone back home who thought I still belonged to him.

"You don't belong to anyone, Devan," he said.

Those words have stuck with me for years. I wish I'd believed them then or at so many points in the years which passed after that night.

My head spun. He didn't want to be second place or wait for me to get my life together. He would've understood if I'd told him upfront, but I didn't. We argued. I cried. He looked away and swiped at his cheek as if maybe he shed a tear, too, but he never let me see his face. He drove me back to the dorm, and as soon as I walked in, Luke was calling, of course. Where had I been, were there guys, was I okay, how were my classes? He was in poor-pitiful-me mode.

I felt sorry for him. I had lied. More than once. There was no actual proof he had lied to me or done anything other than want to protect me. I lost John because of dishonesty. In that moment of defeat, rather than summon the courage to take back my life and start fresh, I defaulted into our routine, and we stayed together for two more years without my attempting to see anyone else.

In the three years we spent together, I became a different person. My parents eventually had to be told about our relationship (from the safety of the other side of my 18th birthday), which, to say the least, was not well received. It was a defining, hurtful moment in our parent/child relationship that helped me mature, but it was full of hard lessons for which I'm now both quite regretful and quite thankful. My lessons weren't all sexual – I was also learning to advocate for myself, to say, "This is what I want. I'm making my own path, regardless of whether it's what others want for me. I'm going to make my own mistakes."

And I did. I made *plenty*.

I made good choices, too, with which others didn't necessarily agree, but they were my choices to make. My relationship with my parents continued through remarkably rocky times, as did my relationship with Luke. Somehow, we stayed together for three long years before I graduated from college and moved to Texas, which ultimately sent us in separate directions. To say I was devastated doesn't begin to define that period of my life.

One day shortly after I moved nearly three years to the day after we started seeing each other, he stopped taking my calls. No warning. No explanation. Earlier that year, he had moved several states away to work with his father and save money to get a place for us to live when we got married. He was originally from that area, so we had always discussed living there.

When he moved back, I didn't question it. He paid my airfare to come visit for eight days that summer, and being in a fast-paced city was like being in a world I didn't realize existed. We had a great time reconnecting after time apart, and when I came back to college to finish school, I did so with the understanding that after just a few more months apart, we would be together forever. Not long before graduation, our plans were thrown a curveball when I got the chance to interview for the job that took me to Texas. He seemed ecstatic.

"Go for it," he told me. "I've always wanted to live out there. It's a beautiful area, and I wouldn't mind getting away from down here. Get us a place to live, and I'll join you."

He didn't come home at Thanksgiving. Then, he didn't come home at Christmas. A week later, he stopped taking my calls. I went into shock. My life became a cycle of going to work, stopping for fast food on the way home, lying on my couch in a dark living room watching TV, and jumping to answer the phone on the first ring in the hope it might be him only to find that, once again, it never was.

I cried in the shower. I cried myself to sleep. I cried on the way to work and again on the trip home each evening. I tried not to cry when I saw couples in the grocery store or heard love songs on the radio. I stared into the dark night after night trying to make out individual ceiling tiles in my tiny apartment bedroom while suffering through the most boringly monotonous, predictably patterned but obnoxiously loud sex routine from the next-door neighbors whose bedroom – and the head of their bed – backed right up to my own. My parents worried about me (why wouldn't they – *I* was worried about me). They came to Texas to check on me a couple of months later when I still wasn't pulling myself together.

"Find some friends," they said. "Visit that nice church across the street and meet some people your age."

They never mentioned Luke while they were in town, but their concern was clear. Getting past the depression of losing the person I considered to be my true love felt impossible, and I genuinely believed I would never replace him. Every day at work, I dialed his number at least 20 times, sometimes more, not even really sure of what I wanted to happen.

I was numb from the pain I was putting myself through, and even if he had miraculously said he wanted me back, it wouldn't have healed the openly pulsing wound I had allowed my life to become. My obsession with finding out why he stopped calling so abruptly went on for six months until one day his brother answered the phone and forced him to talk to me.

He explained he had been seeing a counselor to deal with issues related to his parents' divorce and ongoing issues with his father, and his counselor told him to let go of everything in his past and start fresh. Since I was part of that past, he let me go, too. When he let go, he met someone. I tried to tell myself he let go and then met her, but I honestly didn't know which came first or if it really mattered.

Blah. Blah. Blah. *Excuses.*

I didn't even care.

Just like that, right there on the phone, I let him go just as he had let me go, without warning, without hesitation, without further care or concern. I suppose I only needed to hear his voice and know that I could start breathing again, could be free, could let go of his grip on my life.

So, I decided to be okay with being okay. And I was.

Sitting there in my office with coworkers walking up and down the hall going about their day, talking, working, typing, buzzing around the office, completely unaware I was falling apart so I could try to fall back together, I closed my eyes and held my breath until I nearly fell from my desk chair. When I finally exhaled and took a profoundly bottomless breath back in, it was like inhaling fresh air for the first time in three and a half years.

I was new. Slightly tarnished, painfully tired, and desperately frustrated but transformed, and the door to all the pain had finally closed. What was waiting on the other side was anyone's guess.

Telling my story with Luke may seem like a typical first love lost, but the reality is so much more. Understanding my time with Luke is critical to understanding what followed in my life, not just immediately thereafter, but for years to come. I didn't mourn the loss and move on as I should have. It actually didn't occur to me until I started writing this book how intensely affected I was and how I allowed the loss of that relationship, even as flawed as it was, to linger for years and affect me in ways I didn't understand.

Knowing the person I was before I met him, during our relationship, and after he abandoned our three-year engagement is vital to understanding the state I found myself in alone in Texas and how I made some of my decisions over the following years. I was still the small-town girl from Southeast Arkansas with big dreams and her heart on her sleeve, but the sleeve was hanging by a thread, and the heart was shattered and in dire need of healing attention. I wish I could say I emerged from mourning the end of our relationship stronger and ready to face the world with a mended heart and clear mind, but that was not the case.

"Barely a day passes that I don't hear the words my attacker said to me that night pinging from one side of my head to the other. First, I hear it in one ear. Then, I hear it in the other ear. I can still hear his voice, the exact tone he used, where he placed the emphasis on each word, the slightly whispered harshness with which he said them, the way he was slightly out of breath..."

Chapter Three

Flipping Pages

Not long after my story with Luke turned the page to a new chapter, Donny brooded into my life. I took my parents' advice and ventured over to the nice church across the street, where I met a handful of friends and Donny, a recovering alcoholic who was as needy as I was and nearly two decades my senior.

We met at a get-together at our Sunday School teachers' home. The following week, we ran into each other at our apartment mail-boxes and discovered we lived directly across the courtyard from each other. I still hadn't met many people outside work, and after a few minutes of surface-level conversation, he invited me over to watch a movie. Pretty soon, we were hanging out fairly regularly.

We never crossed any sexual lines, but there was a great deal of closeness. He liked his shoulders and back to be rubbed, and I found if I just stayed close to him and frequently touched him in small, caring ways and took care of him by doing things like cooking and

"

holding his hand, he invited me over, which meant I didn't have to be alone with my sadness.

I wanted to be wanted. He wanted someone to do things for him, even though he never once offered to do anything for me. As a recovering alcoholic, he keyed in on the fact that we might have a problem after this went on for a while and bought me a book called *Codependent No More* by Melody Beattie.

I took my hurt feelings and retreated back to the familiarity of sadness in the confines of my apartment, but after a month or so, I found the courage to call one afternoon to ask if he wanted to go to a movie. Like *out*. For a *real* date. Not hanging out being dysfunctional and sulky in his apartment together.

He said very matter-of-factly, as if I should have already known, that because I was overweight he didn't want anyone to see us and think we were together.

Wow. I had to take a difficult minute to process what he was telling me as I sat on the edge of my bed listening to him on the other end of the telephone.

He was fine with creeping around in his apartment, but he didn't want to be seen with me in public. My feelings were hurt so badly by how he made me feel that I vowed right then and there to lose the weight and never let anyone hurt my feelings again about how I looked. Just as when Luke wrote me off after three years, I once again found myself crying myself to sleep over a man who didn't think enough of me to care one way or another how the things he said or did made me feel. This time, though, I was more on the angry side of tears than sad, and I was determined not to ever let another person make me feel bad about my body.

Donny bruised my spirit, but I'm thankful he did. It hurt straight through to my soul's seeds to hear him say he didn't want to be seen in public with me. This tenderhearted, still-naïve, small-town Southern girl wiped away the tears and vowed to make changes and show him and Luke and every guy who had ignored me what they were missing. I eventually lost the weight and lived a much healthier lifestyle. When I ran into him at the grocery store one night with the man who later became my first husband, Donny couldn't hide the fact that he nearly had to pick his jaw up off the floor when he saw me. Going to a movie with me probably didn't seem like such a bad idea at that moment.

Around that same time, someone came into my life who, to this day, is one of my best friends. Michelle had recently divorced an abusive husband and was raising two girls on her own. She was, and still is, as outspoken, straightforward, and just-when-you-need-it hilarious as the day is long. She was exactly what I needed to wrench me out of the darkness of depression and despair and set me back on the pursuit of light and life.

Despite my misery with Luke and weirdness with Donny, I was still fundamentally the same sheltered girl who believed most people were trustworthy and guys who would lie to me were the exception and not the rule. Michelle convinced me to try out a local club that played '70s and '80s music every Friday night. Our second or third time there, I was waiting in line to fill out a new membership card as a dark-haired, sly-grinned cutie approached. Our county was dry, so alcohol could be served only if you had a "membership," and I had accidentally left mine at home.

"Can you help me fill this out?" he asked, flashing that slightly sideways grin I would soon find heart-poundingly, eyelash-flutter-ingly, answer-stutteringly difficult to deny.

He plopped his membership form on the counter in front of me and handed me a pen. His friends were going in without him and rolled their eyes as they showed their tattered, obviously often-used mem-bership cards. I wondered why his friends had cards that looked as if they had been there many times and this guy didn't have one at all.

"Sure," I replied, uncertain as to why he couldn't do it himself. "What's your name?"

"Will Berry. What's yours?"

I started writing his name and noticed he had a membership card in his hand. A light bulb flickered on over my head.

He's hitting on me! What do I say?
By helping him fill out his membership application
I have his name, phone number, address, and age,
and he has an opening line to talk to me.
What a slick little move...

Surprisingly, he didn't try to take me home that night despite the fact that we talked several times and visually stalked each other around the club. He bought me a drink and showed plenty of interest, and we danced together a couple of times. Later that week, I called him and asked if he wanted to get together.

"I was wondering what took you so long. I figured you would call the next day," he said.

The next evening, he came to my apartment. We hung out, talked, laughed, and had a nice evening. He was exceedingly affectionate, acting as if we had been comfortably coupled for quite a while. I was mostly at ease with him. We relaxed and acted as if we knew each other well but with the slight edge of a relationship that still had that awkward excitability of something new. After much pressure from him to move to a more intimate, physical stage in the evening – and conflicted resistance on my part – he pulled out the "I really see a future for us" speech.

I was hooked.

If I could watch a video of that moment, there would surely be glittery stars and sequined hearts floating above my head as Cupid *thwacked* my heart with a quiver of sparkling arrows.

Clearly, he loved me. *Right? Right?!?*

So, of course, we slept together. It was magical and perfect, and in my overly dramatic mind, it was playing out in slow motion with its own soundtrack and a highlight reel that would play over again in my mind several times in the following days.

As he left, he kissed me so sweetly on the forehead, took my hand in his and kissed it while looking me in the eye and thanking me for a wonderful time, walked backwards out the apartment door, and never broke eye contact. He got to the top of the stairs and turned around one more time to seal the deal with a final sideways-smiling, heart-swooningly charming look, and turned toward the stairs with the promise of, "I'll call you."

And, of course, he didn't.

I had his phone number, though, and his address. Big mistake on his part. BIG. In my naiveté and immaturity, I made an all-out fool of myself for the next month driving by to see if his car was at his apartment, calling his phone, and even going right up to his door one day to ask to see him. His roommate shook his head, rolled his eyes, and told me in so many words, "You got played. Don't come back here."

I was devastated. Will had said and done all the right things. Didn't he say he saw a future for us? Why would he say all those things if he didn't mean them? Why would he sleep with me if he didn't want to be with me? It sounds so ridiculous now, but I actually wondered these things to myself and didn't understand the answers. I moped around for a few days and was on the beginning downhill slide of a Luke-level depression when Michelle met me for lunch and told me life wasn't like the movies and to quit expecting it to be. She said the way he acted that morning when he left my apartment didn't make him a romantic guy – it made him a "player," and I was a victim of "the game."

"Get over it, sister," she said. "So, you got played. Big deal. You live, and you learn. There's lots of fish in the sea. Put on that cute skirt you bought last week, stick your head back in the water, make a cute fishy face, and get you another one."

I sat there listening to what she was saying, and, at first, I rejected it. This couldn't be how the world really was. Not *my* world. My world was built on a foundation of impeccable report cards, big dreams from an early age, the "golden touch" my parents had always claimed I had, a career that was taking off, small-town morals, and a love of family and faith that ran as deep as the expectation of manners and respect my parents had instilled in me. My world couldn't be this cynical and cruel.

But as long as I have fun and don't get close to anyone,
nobody can hurt me.
I was with Luke my senior year of high school
and all through college.
It's my turn to relax, have fun, and be young.

As much as I didn't want to hear what she was saying, something about her words made sense. Something changed in me that day, as if someone flipped a switch, and the naïve girl who so desperately wanted her heart back in one piece decided to worry less about her heart and think more about fun. So, I took Michelle's advice and ran with it.

And, boy, did I run. I got quite good at it actually. It got easier and easier to love them and move on. In fact, love never really seemed to be required.

Redheaded Joseph was entertaining and enjoyed public displays of affection and the same movies and music I did. He was also quite fond of a general lack of commitment, which worked out great when it was time to move on sans warning to flippy-haired, blond delivery guy James who happened into the office one day when I was wearing that aforementioned cute skirt and an equally sassy attitude. He was as dumb as a box of headless hammers but easy on the eyes and unpredictably, set-you-up-on-your-dryer-to-kiss-you exciting.

Short, dark-haired, saxophone-playing Joshua actually saved me from going home with Will one night when Will came creeping around the club. Joshua must have sensed I was torn between wanting to talk to this guy and run out in tears. He stepped up beside me, put his arm around me, and said, "There you are," pulled me in close, looked over my shoulder and glared at Will, who promptly got the message and left, never to be heard from or seen again in my life. Joshua, on the other hand, became a fairly regular fixture for the next couple of weeks until we both accepted that his band's schedule kept him away too much. I replaced him with lanky, inexperienced Tate, who had more than enough know-how on the dance floor but little to no practice with women.

You would think as quickly as those months went by, the guys would blur from one to the next, but I was quite fond of them all and relished the moments we shared, so all these years later, they each stand out to me in unique ways. Unlike others who interact with various people and experience different things without allowing the experiences to become significant to them, I still recall each one as very defining. They were each a minor part of the person I was evolving into, the young woman who was beginning to live and take chances, smile more, and stop worrying what the rest of the world thought.

The girl who had done everything she had ever been told to do and had made every "A" she was supposed to make and been home on time and followed every rule and been to every club meeting and turned in every homework assignment and worried every worry was on her own and making her own mistakes and most importantly – very, very, oh-so-very importantly – she was okay with that.

If these men were mistakes, *let them be*. Maybe it was time to be full of mistakes and fall and get back up and move on.

And *breathe*.

I had held my breath for so many years worried over what other people thought, and for the first time in my life, I found myself concerned solely with what I wanted and needed, and that was truly, 100%, without-a-doubt okay.

I was okay.

I didn't need a man. I enjoyed having one around, but I didn't really *need* one. For the first time, I was standing on my own two feet and not steadily looking for someone to fill a gap or to define me as a person.

My world wasn't perfect, of course. I definitely wasn't living the life my parents had dreamed of for the "lady" they thought they'd raised. At that point, it did seem the guys started blurring together faster than I could slam the door behind them, although there were certainly a great many people who had more experiences. Compared to the sheltered, relatively innocent life I had led to that point, though, I felt out of control, as if I were freewheeling my way through the world without looking back. Even so, I giggled a little wondering what everyone back home – and Luke, of course – would think if they knew.

I enjoyed my fun-seeking, short-skirted life, thumbing my nose at anything and anyone who wanted to control me or limit me in any way until the day I stumbled across a personals ad and took a dare to meet someone.

Cue the sound of screeching brakes on the freewheeling life…

CHAPTER FOUR

'Til Death or Dishonesty Do Us Part

The blue-eyed, dark-haired guy who bounded around the corner and nearly knocked me down that night I took a dare and drove an hour and a half to Mesquite, Texas, ended up walking along the shore of Lake Tawakoni with me until sunrise. About a week later, he showed up at my door with a box of personal items and never fully left again. Three months later, he asked me to marry him, and I said, "Yes," despite the countless red flags foreshadowing my mistake.

Yep. I married the first guy who halfway showed interest.

Everyone my age was getting married. It felt like what I was supposed to do. There was a guy who wanted to make an honest woman out of me. Shouldn't I pick out timelessly lovely china patterns, be the dutiful daughter and have smile-even-though-you-don't-know-these-people bridal showers, go overpriced-wedding-dress shopping, choose from more flowers than I'd ever seen in one place, send elegantly within-budget invitations, politely shake my parents' friends' hands at the reception while thanking them for never-to-be-used gravy boats and cloth napkins, and stroll hand-in-hand with Mr. Right into marital bliss?

I was 22 years old and, by small-town standards, not getting any younger. Of course, I should take advantage of this chance to settle down, and that's exactly what I did. Considering the ongoing revolving-door mess my life had become, my conscience told me it was the right thing to do even though I was quite fond of the independence I had cultivated.

Mr. Right was unfortunately Mr. Wrong, which I discovered the evening of day one of becoming Mrs. Wrong when he yelled at me like a rabid dog in the street on our wedding night because our hotel didn't have the specific room he wanted. From there, his unpredictability escalated quickly. I never knew how he would greet me each day when I returned home from work.

Would there be another new person living in our home for whom I was expected to cook and clean? He frequently rotated various strangers through our home, sometimes two at a time, giving them free rent and board in exchange for working with him in his repo business, and I wasn't allowed to question his choices, even though I didn't always feel safe with some of the people he chose.

Would this be the day he threw something across the room again? One day, it was a spoonful of spaghetti sauce against the kitchen wall when I asked if he could give me money to help with bills in a very non-confrontational way specifically designed to, in fact, avoid spoon-throwing types of behavior. I was left to clean up the red, dripping mess, and dinner ended up in the refrigerator because he and the guy he had moved in stormed out of the house and didn't come back until the middle of the night, at which point he smelled like alcohol, cigarettes, and another woman as he crawled into bed with the usual, "I'm sorry about earlier, but you just make me so mad sometimes."

Another day, it was a shoe that narrowly missed me as it flew past my head and hit the bedroom wall. When I found the courage later to bring up the flying shoe incident in front of one of his employees who was living with us, Mr. Wrong laughed and swore the shoe was supposed to land in the closet. On the day he threw it, he certainly hadn't been laughing. He was in the middle of raising his voice at me just enough so no one else in the house could hear him as he made his point that he would give me money for bills if and when he felt ready. Of course, he was quick to make a joke about it in front of this other person to defuse the conversation. As usual, he was brilliant at deflecting attention from himself and casting that spotlight onto what he labeled as my "overreactions and nagging."

Financially, he took but rarely contributed, and I later discovered one of his girlfriends had signed my name to things that hadn't been paid, including a rental car that wasn't left in good condition on one of their weekend trips to Dallas. After we divorced, he refused to make payments on the truck I had bought him. When the credit union said they were coming to repossess it, he removed the tires, put it up on cinder blocks, smashed the windows with a sledgehammer, and partially burned it.

From an outsider's perspective, we probably appeared reasonably happy during our marriage because he was a pro at seeming like a decent guy, and my pride was big enough to disguise an endless array of marital shortcomings. Mr. Wrong cheated on me mercilessly throughout our marriage, even bringing other women into our home and our bed while I was out of town and not trying to hide it when I returned.

He moved us to an older rent house in a remote, rundown part of town that was primarily a business district. The closest neighbors were at least a block away, and I was on the opposite side of a fairly large town from anyone I knew. He did all he could to isolate me from the life I'd established before we married. Emotional, mental, and verbal warfare were an everyday thing in our home, although he was an expert at hiding it in front of our friends and family and even in front of the guys he moved into our home.

One of the guys, Dwayne, later told me that Mr. Wrong claimed I was cheating on him with one of the physicians at the hospital where I worked, so he felt he was more than justified when he cheated. When Dwayne came back to the house by himself one night and found me sitting by the phone, he realized what he had been told about me was lies and told me the truth about Mr. Wrong's cheating.

"What are you doing?" he asked.

"Just hanging out," I replied.

"No, I mean why do you have the phone by you?" he said. "You waitin' on a call from somebody? Maybe your boyfriend?"

I remember laughing and looking at him as if he must be joking. When I saw the serious look on his face, I was horrified that he might actually think that could be true.

"I sit here like this every night waiting on my *husband* to call," I told him. "Sometimes he calls before I go to bed, and if this is going to be one of those nights, I don't want to miss it."

Dwayne stopped dead in his tracks and just about had to pick his mouth up off the floor. The story of all that Mr. Wrong had been up to started spilling out, and my world turned upside down. I suppose I already knew on some level but didn't want to accept that he could be so heartless. Despite the ongoing issues in our marriage, I still wanted to believe he was a good person who had simply never had a chance to know what a decent, happy marriage and life looked like, and, if given the chance, he would mature into the husband I needed him to be.

The next night, I drove by the home of the girl Mr. Wrong was supposedly cheating with, and, true to Dwayne's story, there was his truck backed in under her carport trying to hide when he was supposed to be out working. Seeing it with my own eyes was harder than I'd imagined it would be. Even though I thought I'd already accepted what I was going to see, actually seeing his truck there made it real.

What are they doing in there?
Is he giving her all the 'I love yous'
and smiles and hugs and kisses
he's supposed to be giving me?
What is he telling her about me?

I am More

*Is he telling her I'm dead like he told the
girl from San Antonio
he flirted with online after we first got married?*

He thought I didn't know about the other girls, and perhaps those online flirtations didn't go anywhere. Maybe this hadn't yet gone anywhere either, but clearly, he was attempting to take it *somewhere*. He was hiding. He was lying. He was pursuing this woman while married to me and while he'd told me he was working.

That truck backed in under that carport belonged to my husband, and this home belonged to another woman. Any type of relationship he was in was inappropriate regardless of the circumstances.

I was angry, disappointed, sad, embarrassed. I sat in my Mustang in the middle of the road outside this woman's house alternately leaning back in the seat sobbing and leaning forward screaming while I beat the steering wheel until my hands were red and sore. Anger and frustration and embarrassment were pouring out of every broken part of me, and for the first time I was unpacking my limitless, neatly compartmentalized feelings and letting them all out to ache at once.

A few minutes into my sobbing, screaming tirade, I was numb both mentally and physically. I put the car in gear and floored it out of the neighborhood cresting both speedbumps at top speed on the way out. Dwayne had told me he would be at his girlfriend's house a couple of miles away if I needed him. I barely hit the brakes as I slid into his girlfriend's driveway sideways, kicked the car door open, and stumbled across the yard to the steps.

I didn't even have to knock. They rushed to the door when they heard me come flying into the yard.

"She saw him," he said, flinging the screen door open and rushing down the steps in time to catch me as I collapsed.

He helped me to my feet, and all I could think to say as he helped me into the house was, "He's there. His truck is there."

"I know, sweetie," Dwayne said. "I'm so sorry."

His girlfriend just shook her head and offered me a comfortable place on the couch. I was in shock. I could hear them talking about me, but everything sounded muffled as if I were in a deep cave with a series of heavy doors between me and the rest of the world. After a while, sound filtered in, and my burning reality began to feel good through the haze. The piercing, the stabbing, the pulsing, the stinging – in a bizarre way, I needed to feel all of it, to submerge in it, to figure out who I was in this new truth.

After a while, I could hear clearly, but all those intense feelings stopped, and the numbness set back in. Among the first words I heard was Dwayne's shock at seeing me standing up suddenly to leave.

"Where are you going? You can't go," he said, clearly worried about what I might do if left unsupervised.

"I have things to do," I said. "I need to get busy. Don't worry. I'm not going to kill him."

Neither of them seemed to take much comfort in those words as I marched out the door to my car, but I promised to call him the following day to check in. Realizing Mr. Wrong would know who told me about his girlfriend, Dwayne had already removed his personal things from our home with no plans to return. Still dazed, I drove home assessing how I could best begin to heal my wounded pride and reconcile my pre-marriage self with the new person I was now forced to be.

Thankfully, I made it home about an hour before Mr. Wrong came in dripping with kind words and loving gestures as he often did when he had been with another woman. Throughout our marriage to that point, I'd hoped those were times when he remembered how much he loved me and how much he missed the nights when we used to go out looking for cars together before he had people who worked for him. After seeing his truck backed into her carport and hearing Dwayne's accounts of his exploits, I realized those were nights he got lucky or nights he was trying to balance his sins with compassion to clear his conscience.

I watched him that night bouncing around our home in such a good mood, and I became dizzy from suppressing the stress. The words I'd said to Dwayne echoed through my mind.

Don't worry. I'm not going to kill him.

There was a loaded 9mm in my nightstand that could have so easily taken care of my broken heart, and I was numb enough to not care what happened to me after it was over. The way he always made me feel, the way he talked to me, the way he isolated me, the way I had felt when I saw him at her house backed in and hiding his truck, the way I'd sat in the road screaming and beating the steering wheel, the way I'd fallen out of the car and stumbled across the yard, the way my skin had crawled when he touched me that night when he came home…

I locked myself in the bathroom, sat on the edge of the bathtub, wrapped my arms around myself, and cried until the suffocating feeling of desperation passed. He hadn't done anything to deserve to die, I didn't truly want him to, and I probably couldn't have pulled the trigger, even if I had been bold enough to aim the gun. I sat in the bathroom that night praying to God to give me strength to know what to do and to rid me of the desire to use the gun on myself rather than on him to escape this world in which I was trapped, this world I had no idea how I had arrived in but that I knew was not where I wanted to be.

The following morning, I awoke with the intense feeling that I was living in a new space both within myself and within my home. Life looked filtered, changed. Looking around, I saw things with new eyes, as if I could understand them clearly for the first time in such a long time. I knew exactly what I needed to do and how to do it from the minute my eyes opened as if my life's plan had been downloaded straight to my brain while I slept through the power of the previous night's desperate, pleading prayers.

I enlisted the help of about a dozen friends, including Dwayne and his girlfriend, to strip the house in two hours flat to nothing but the things Mr. Wrong had brought into the marriage and the things we purchased together – never let it be said I wasn't reasonable. I even took his clothes off the hangers and took the hangers with me. While I wanted to be fair, I wasn't leaving without being very clear about my feelings.

As an extra step toward making sure he knew exactly how I felt about his abuse and betrayal, I took one of his prized possessions – the custom groom's cake topper my parents ordered in the likeness of his tow truck – and smashed it into so many pieces it was nearly unrecognizable. I placed it in the middle of our bare dining room floor where he would be forced to walk past it. As I walked out the door to leave with the trailer full of everything from the house, I left a kiss-my-scalded-butt, forget-you-ever-knew-me, get-my-name-out-of-your-mouth letter right on top of the shattered pieces.

Unfortunately, anyone who knows me well enough could have told you I would stupidly go back to the house that night. They all warned me not to go. They said it wasn't safe, and I agreed. I didn't intend to go back, but after the last load was secured at the storage building and I had stopped by to introduce myself to the girlfriend and tell her she could have him but that she should know what she was getting into, I returned to the house to pick up my cat and dog, expecting him to still be at the bar.

I didn't expect him to beat me back to the house. The door was partially open, and I could see his silhouette coming around the corner from the dining room to the living room. He was still in his going-out clothes, only now he had the added accessory of a shotgun by his side. When I pushed the door open a little further, he greeted me with the shotgun directly to my face.

"What the hell do you want? What're you doing here?" he barked.

"Please put the gun down," I said. "Please don't do this. I'm begging you."

My hands shook, and my feet and knees were so locked into that spot, I don't know if I could have run away if I had the courage. All I could do was wonder how quickly it would be over and how many times he would shoot me before I died. He didn't back down right away, even though he could see that it was me, that I was scared, that I was unarmed, and that I didn't intend him any harm. He finally dropped the gun to his side, but it was quite a while before he put it away, even though I asked him to.

Moments like that are memories that don't fade easily. No matter how much living I'd done up to that point, I wasn't made for screaming arguments with the man who was supposed to love me. Every time he gestured with the shotgun, I jumped, and a few times I broke into tears.

He finally asked, "Do you think I'm going to shoot you or something?"

I stared back at him, afraid to answer. I didn't know what to say. If I had answered honestly, I would have said I didn't know what he was capable of and that I had been walking on eggshells around him for so long that my tears were about more than the gun. Instead, I answered with silence and stood in front of him shaking and upset, afraid to look at him but afraid to look anywhere else.

He put the gun on the living room floor just out of reach, but still where I could see it, and softened around the edges ever so slightly. Something in him changed a little, as if he saw *me* for the first time in that moment – not the woman who cleaned out his home while he was gone, smashed one of his prized mementos, and came back to take his pets. In that moment, he talked to me as if I were the woman who married him, who took care of him when he was sick and cooked his meals so many times, who faithfully continued asking about his day even though he rarely took the time to do anything but ignore her.

The hours that followed were bizarre. I was broken. I told him exactly how he had made me feel all those months I spent tiptoeing across the eggshells of our separate lives trying not to disrupt what little balance there might be from one minute to the next. For the first time, I held back very little, and somehow through the accusations and tears, he agreed. We sat on the floor in our bare living room and wept together. Neither one of us knew what to say or how to act. We only knew we were wounded – both as individuals and as a couple – and that it would not soon go away.

We talked, we yelled, we cried, we got in each other's faces. We even laughed a few times in softer moments when we were talking and being reasonable. He admitted seeing the girl I knew about and several I had wondered about, and I flashed back to a call I received from his first wife not long after we got married warning me that this was exactly what was going to happen, that this was his pattern of behavior, and that he wouldn't stop no matter how good I was to him or what kind of home and life I tried to make for us.

I can't win.
Nothing I ever do for this man will be good enough.
She was right.

She warned me,
But by the time she told me all those things,
it was already too late.
Now, all this. What do I do?

My answer was to give him another chance. We had been married only six months, and my pride and determination were too out of control to give up. I had to know if we could make it work. No matter how terrible things seemed as we sat on the floor in the middle of the night in our bare living room with the emotions of our stripped-down relationship hanging palpably in the air, a shotgun prominently within reach of my cheating husband, and my face stained from more tears than I knew were possible, if I had waved the white flag that soon, I would've spent the rest of my life wondering if our marriage could have been saved.

In my pride-filled immaturity, I still thought I loved this man and needed him, just as I thought I needed Luke before him. He didn't make excuses or try to apologize for what he had done or for how he had treated me during our brief marriage, but I still felt myself wanting to reach out and embrace him. I wanted to hold him so close that no trouble or heartache could wedge between us. I wanted to feel the person I thought I'd fallen in love with rising up to meet my touch. Instead, we continued sitting, staring into space, crying tears that felt as if they poured directly from my heart.

The need for sleep began to outweigh the need to keep analyzing the relationship. Exhaustion began to set in, and he asked where I planned to stay. Stupidly, I told him, and before I could make myself stop talking, I offered to let him join me. The part of me that cared enough about this man to marry him couldn't stand to leave him on the living room floor, and the immature, jealous part of me knew as long as he was near my side, he couldn't be with another woman. At that point, I knew, no matter how hard I tried to deny it and no matter how much I bristled and raged about being hurt, he still held my mental and emotional controls in his palm.

When we arrived at the hotel, I was so exhausted from frustration that I let him check me in. We pulled around to the room, brought in my suitcase, and stared at each other for what seemed like eternity.

"I'll sleep on the floor." He twisted the knife a little deeper in my heart as we both stared at the cheap, worn carpet.

I searched deep inside myself for an answer. The one that came out shocked us both.

"You can sleep here," I said, gesturing at the king-sized bed. "It's okay. After all, we're still married. For now."

I felt as if I died a lingeringly excruciating death and leapt directly onto the expressway to Hell. Having him lie in the bed beside me made me nauseous, but, undeniably, I could hear a small voice in my head reminding me how much I wanted him to love me and how much I wanted him to be happy. I thought my pain and fear would at least muffle the squeak of that annoying little voice. Instead, it got louder and more insistent.

You should cut him some slack.
You aren't that easy to live with.
You're jumping to conclusions.
Why didn't you confront him
and give him a chance to explain?
Why didn't you trust him more?
Why do you always have to be so dramatic?
You're the cause of all this.
Why do you get yourself into these situations?
Why?

We woke up around the same time the next morning staring at each other, strangers with a common bond of memories. We explored each other's eyes searching for sane reasoning, but we only found a long-ago-lost but still deeply rooted attraction and the remembrance of better days. Without a word, he closed the gap between us, moving to lie on the bed closely beside me for the first time in longer than I could recall. He kissed me so gently and honestly, I sensed, for just a moment, the blush of how it felt to kiss him a lifetime of nights ago for the first time on the banks of Lake Tawakoni.

Before either of us knew what was happening, we were holding each other, and we made love. Right there in the room that was supposed to be my haven from reality and my escape from him for a few days as I pondered whether to file for a divorce, we made love as we never had before: like a married couple who truly wanted to be together. When it was over, our eyes locked into a deeply seeking, uncomfortable hold. I jerked away and hid my face.

"What's wrong?" he asked, as if for the first time he actually cared.

He was answered with tears. I cried until my whole body shook. I cried tears that had built up for months. He didn't know how to respond as he held me and looked at me with a face that silently pleaded to know what to do or what to say, how to act in this impossible situation. After several minutes, he finally spoke the only thing he could think of to make me feel better.

"It'll be okay," he said. "Everything will be okay."

All I could answer him with were averted eyes and tears he knew he created. As much as I thought I wanted to be with him when he kissed me and as much as I wanted him to want me in that moment, I looked at him when it was over and wondered,

Did you hold her like that?
Did you do that to her?
How did she kiss you?
Are you going to see her again?
Will you think of this moment?
Will you share a laugh about it?

It occurred to me lying there in the hotel with my semi-estranged, cheating husband that I didn't want to have sex with him that morning, although certainly when he kissed me so lovingly, my brain had defaulted to what I thought was a caring place. I really only wanted him to want me as he wanted his other girls, to see me how he saw them in a way that made him happy, that made him smile and relax and be less angry and tense, and if that meant giving him my body, then I could lie there and be with him.

While we were together in those moments, I felt my own peace and happiness, but when it was over, tears and frustration welled up, and the anxiety of the six months of our marriage draped itself over me. I was allowing my body to be used to try to grasp onto some semblance of a marriage, but I didn't want my husband to want me because of that.

I did not like the person I had become.

I grew up in a two-parent home wrapped in hugs, nightly prayer, personal expectations of behavior and academic success, and an appreciation for what it means to treat people with compassion and love.

He grew up mostly in a boys' home with inconsistent family interactions, alcoholism, and a string of other issues. Suffice it to say, his childhood wasn't what you would call ideal, and it did not translate nicely into the model husband I wanted to wake up across the bed from every morning. In fact, most mornings, I woke up alone since he was gone so much, and even when he was home, I was still alone for all practical purposes.

Lying there being held and comforted by this man who felt like a stranger, I realized not wanting to be alone was what sent me down the aisle to say "I do." A few months later, here I was in a hotel room wishing for nothing but solitude and escape from him, and I had not only let him share the room, but he was also lying next to me, holding me, and reassuring me about the tears he fostered. I struggled to push that depressing realization aside.

He didn't do this, Devan.
You did.
You're such a helpless wreck.
Get up, and either fix it or be done with it.
Either way, get yourself together.

So that's what I did. I compartmentalized my feelings (again) as much as possible – the embarrassment, the anger, the sadness – and tried to make a new start with a fresh perspective. The idea seemed world-changing to me, but he didn't seem surprised when I announced we should give our marriage a second try. After a couple of nights in the hotel, we started a trial separation, which mostly meant he lived in the back of the house, and I lived in the front of the house on a mattress we moved back from the storage building.

After about three weeks of being "separated," we tried to get back together, but the root issues persisted. You can't force someone with abusive tendencies who chronically cheats to give up his ways if he likes what he's doing any more than you can force a rose-colored-glasses-wearing girl from a good family to give up her dream of sharing life with someone who loves and respects her.

After a few months of putting on brave faces and pretending to have a stable marriage and make things work, we had several defining experiences that placed our relationship on the final approach to divorce. He made a jerk out of himself at my graduate school graduation, and I didn't quietly keep the peace as I previously might have. I let him know in no uncertain terms that I wished he had stayed home so that day would be a memory I didn't share with him. It also did not escape his attention that my maiden name was on the program and on my diploma.

When it came time to travel two states away for my brother's high school graduation, he announced the day before that he wasn't going, even though we had bought him new clothes for the occasion and talked about the event at length. I went alone, offered no explanation to my family, and came home to evidence that the new guy who had recently moved into our back room kept a guest for the weekend and that another woman slept in my bed while I was gone. Mr. Wrong didn't bother to answer me when I asked why there were four sets of dishes and why two of the four glasses in the sink had lipstick on them.

We were keenly aware that certain boundaries had been crossed. He knew I would stand up to him, and I knew he was going to give me every chance he could to prove it. There were still peaceful moments, but they were more like moments shared between room-mates: inconsistent episodes not worthy of filing away with better memories.

I came home in the evenings as he was leaving. He came home in the mornings as I made my way out the door. We did what I jok-ingly referred to as the "chance pass-n-peck," an occasional kiss on the cheek as we passed in the driveway, more of a formality really than genuine sentiment. I became accustomed to living alone again and found my resolve to not be his doormat strengthening daily. I developed the ability to hover above the relationship and see its faults, a skill I had suppressed for too long. All the things I had denied became increasingly apparent.

My unhappiness escalated. Family and friends were aware that the once fun-loving, smiling me was suspiciously absent. No one spoke about our previous separation. Knowing me as they did, they knew it was a closed discussion. Everyone knew there wasn't any argument they could make that would lessen my determination to beat our problems.

Sometimes you have to step outside your circumstances and take a long look around. When I did that, what I saw was someone so far removed from the man to whom I thought I'd committed my life that I barely recognized him. And, looking back, I'm sure he felt the same way about me. Where was the man who had made it his life's mission to make me laugh until I cried or the man who held me and reassured me when my grandmother had health problems? Where was Prince Charming with the heart-melting blue eyes that spoke more with one look than all the romance novels I'd ever read?

Even now, I'm unsure whether it was my stubborn, competitive need to win or my inexplicable love for him that kept me from admitting it was time to move on. I did, however, reach the point where something had to be said. Every time he walked out the door, it got harder to face an empty house and a cold bed. I began sleeping with my arm stretched to his side of the bed so I would know if he came home in the middle of the night. I often stared out the window watching him in the yard, feeling more like a spectator in his life than a wife who wanted even the slightest notice from her husband.

One night, my dam of resistance finally broke.

"We're going to look for a car. Do you want to go with us?" His rare offer was yelled in from the back door. He had one foot out the door already.

"Sure. Let me get my shoes."

"Hurry up" was his only response.

I met him in the yard, and he looked uncomfortable. We hadn't done anything together in a long time, even something as minor as this. I assumed he had expected a "no."

"You can sit in the front seat," I told M.J., the most recent person in the endless string of guys who had shown up in the back room of our home one morning and started working for my husband. I never knew who would be there. Secretly, I didn't feel as if I belonged in that front seat next to my husband or that I would even have been welcome.

We took his latest toy: a purple Camaro with white racing stripes. I folded into the back seat and settled into silence. They talked and listened to the radio. I laid my head back on the seat and began to examine my current situation. Before long, tiny tears of resentment ran down my cheeks. I stared at the back of his head.

Here I am,
sitting in the back of a Camaro late at night
being ignored by my own husband,

and I think he's forgotten I'm here.
What a life.
Who are you? What have you done with
the man I married?
Where is that sweet guy who used to go out of his way
to make sure I was happy?
Where is that goofy grin that peeked at me over a vase
of roses on Valentine's Day?

If you've been there, you know what I felt – that aching hurt known as reality that grabs hold of your heart and starts eating its way toward your brain. That unsettling feeling that you made a mistake. That feeling that usually accompanies the need to run and hide.

Something had to happen. I decided when we got home I would either fix it or end it, one way or another. When we finally got home and the car door swung open, I made it clear I was in a hurry. He caught up with me in the laundry room as I dragged clothes out of the dryer to cover my flurry of emotion.

"What's wrong with you?"

"Nothing," I mumbled. I turned away, trying to hide my tears. "I'm just not happy. I haven't been for a long time."

He grabbed me by the arm, and clothes fell at our feet as he jerked me up to a standing position and swung me around to force me to face him. He could see the tears I'd been trying to hide, and his eyes begged to know what to say as he dropped my arm in shock.

I wish I'd known right then and there what to tell him, but instead, I ran from the room and headed straight for our bedroom, the site of most of our better arguments.

Here it comes.
Now he's going to be mad.

He wasn't, though. He followed me, and for the first time, possibly ever, we talked from the heart, even more honestly than the night he shoved the gun in my face when I tried to leave him. Our conversation was direct. We admitted we didn't know how to fix our marriage. He thought time apart was the answer. I thought that was the worst idea possible. I couldn't stand that we would spend time apart so he could be with other girls while I pined myself away and then took him back after a few weeks. I was tired of relationship games.

"If we separate, that's it," I told him. My brave response surprised us both.

"So, what're you saying? Do you want a divorce?" he asked, unable to hide his surprise.

"I don't want a divorce, but I can't go on living like you're my roommate. I can't go on feeling like this every day and trying to remember what it was like to be happy, and trying to..."

Tears finished my sentence. The sound of our relationship breaking up was audible in the silence that followed. After what seemed like hours, we talked on and decided that when I went on vacation with my family in early August, we would use that as time apart to reevaluate.

Emotionally spent once again, I began my retreat to the one place I was usually able to find a few moments of peace – a hot bath.

"I love you. I hate to see you crying."

I turned slowly, and with all the pains of our relationship having taken their toll, I stood silently in the bathroom doorway for several seconds. I'm sure he must have seen the same strained, pleading look he had shown me so many months earlier looking back at him this time – the look that had begged for me to let go.

"Don't say that," I said. "The reason we got back together in the first place is because you hate to see me cry. Let's not ruin this by making that mistake again, okay?"

Words escaped him. I knew the feeling. For once in my life, I couldn't think of a single thing to say. But my eyes were open, and a strong feeling was growing – a feeling that I could stand on my own feet, a feeling that I should be happy and that getting there was within my reach.

The next few days went well. He told me repeatedly that he loved me, but that was short-lived.

"Where are you going?"

It was night, and he was home. He had been in a talkative mood earlier in the evening but suddenly didn't seem to want to be around me or to talk at all. My question followed him to the kitchen, where he ignored it and promptly let the door swing shut. Knowing he would pass right by the chicken I had left out for dinner, I followed him.

Swinging the kitchen door open, I was greeted by the sound of a metal spoon thrown against the wall behind the stove. One look at his face told me quickly that his temper was raging.

"Dammit! I can't even come in the kitchen without you under my feet! What the hell do you want now?" I didn't stop walking. I spun around and walked right back to the living room. When he followed to see what kind of fight he could start, he was answered with silence.

"So, what?! You're not gonna talk to me now?"

I said nothing.

"Whatever. Bitch."

M.J. witnessed the whole incident and looked the other way, just as everyone else had done for so long. Something surged in me. With all the determination I could muster, I flung the kitchen door back open, making sure it slammed every bit as hard against the opposite wall as he had thrown the spoon.

"For your information, I came in here to tell you that I love you and that since I love you so much, I cooked dinner even though I didn't think you'd be here until later, if you made it home at all. I was thinking about you, even though you *never* think about me, and if you could stop yelling and check your attitude for one minute you might have heard me. I'm sorry I even cared!"

I spun around once more and stomped back into the living room as he stomped out the back door. My hands shook. This amount of courage was foreign to me. I trembled at the thought that he could change so quickly after we had been doing so well and wondered where this left us. He had been so nice all week. How far would this set us back?

The next morning started like any other. The alarm went off, and I woke up by myself, as usual, but keys were clinking in the door. He was home. Not knowing who might be with him, I opted not to rush into the living room in my pajamas. It didn't take long for him to join me in the bedroom with something obviously on his mind. Considering how we had parted the night before, I tried to keep the conversation light.

"What time do you want to leave for my parents' house next week?"

This was a topic I knew he would gladly discuss. For several months, we had been planning to spend the Fourth of July at my aunt and uncle's house, and he eagerly anticipated the fireworks, festivities, and fun that always surrounded these family gatherings.

"I don't think I'm going." He didn't look at me.

"What? What do you mean you're not going?"

"I'm not going. I have a lot to do here."

We argued. I reminded him these plans weren't new, that I couldn't recall a time when he hadn't backed out on the things I tried to plan for us to do together, and that it was important for our marriage that we spend time together.

That's when he said it.

"I never intended to go with you, Devan."

He finally made eye contact with me, and I understood. For the first time in more than two years, I honestly woke up. He hadn't planned to be with me by then because the only plans he had didn't include me.

"So, what're you saying?" I asked, tears breaking through my attempt at composure. "Are you saying this is it? Is this the end?"

I barely finished the question. As it had so many times before, the look in his eyes told me all I needed to know.

We yelled. We cried. The truth about how I'd felt for so long came flooding out, and I think he was shocked to hear it all at once. Despite how many times we had argued or how many times we had discussed that things weren't right between us, I don't think he had ever truly considered I might be just as done with the relationship and living with regrets about all the times we tried to fix it as he was.

Suddenly, although I can't say it was without warning, our marriage was over. He stormed out to find boxes for packing, and I was alone in the middle of the kitchen in our rickety old house that I had tried so desperately to make into a home. Somehow amidst the dizzying stress and blood-boiling anger, the most eerily peaceful composure overtook me.

I was determined to stand my ground and force him to leave the house he had never tried to make a home. The first time we separated, I packed in a whirlwind, took my broken heart, and fled. This time, he had to be the one to leave or face trespassing charges. The lease was in my name, not his. The girl who could be swayed by his words and poor-pitiful-me act no longer lived here. It was just me, fiercely tired, savagely focused but sad me, and all I could think of was purging my home of everything that reminded me of him.

First, his clothes, followed by his model cars. Then, his personal items, gun, and games. All went into a pile in the kitchen floor. I wanted everything that was his out of my sight.

By the time he returned, almost everything was in one pile. He grabbed my arm as we passed in the kitchen to get me to slow down. I pushed him away and kept going. I didn't want to talk. I didn't want to think. I didn't want his dirty, other-woman-groping hand grabbing my arm ever again, forcing me to do things.

I just wanted him to leave.

CHAPTER FIVE

Waking Up Lost

That first night was the longest of my life. He was furious when he left, and I'd seen that enraged look before. I couldn't sleep. I couldn't focus. I walked from window to window watching for any sign he was coming back to hurt me.

Three a.m. found me patrolling the sidewalk in front of my house covered in a veil of tears and a thin pair of pajamas with a shaking hand death-gripped on a loaded 9mm. Every time I closed my eyes, I saw his shotgun in my face the night I tried to leave. Even after I coaxed myself off the sidewalk where I'd crumbled into a crying heap and stumbled into the house, I bolted to the windows every time a car came by, prepared to see his truck crashing through.

My life was panic-driven. My thoughts were as scattered as my actions. After three virtually sleepless days and nights, friends who had drifted in and out checking on me talked me into letting them watch over me long enough so that I could sleep without waking up to check the windows every five minutes. The days that followed were tormented with memories of the random good times and a feeling that something could have been different.

One minute I felt as if I could conquer the world with the strength of my newfound freedom. The next minute, I didn't think I could go on without him. I knew divorce was for the best – so many avenues were open that had been closed. I could travel, follow my career wherever it led, dress how I wanted to dress, eat what I wanted to eat, do what I wanted to do.

But somehow, even knowing all that did not make the tears go away.

He popped in and out in the days that followed, which didn't make it any easier to deal with my new reality. I was sure no one could want me now. I was used goods, a leftover from a failed marriage, and he did his best to reinforce that.

I tried to stay in the house and live out the terms of our lease, but he frequently drove by with whatever girlfriend was the flavor of the week to see if another man's car was parked in the driveway. Once, he pulled across four lanes of traffic and nearly crashed into the front of the house, leaving huge ruts in my yard to confront a man who was standing outside. It was the man the landlord had paid to mow the yard (who consequently refused to come back after being so hostilely threatened).

When I finally broke the lease and got an apartment a few months later, he followed me home from work to find out where I lived. He routinely drove by, making sure, of course, that I saw him and heard his loud truck. He regularly asked friends about me to make sure I wasn't dating anyone as if he had some sort of ownership over my life. In typical abuser fashion, he wanted to make sure he retained what he saw as his rightful power, that he could continue to keep me isolated, and that I knew he was watching and constantly aware of every move I made.

As weird as it might sound, even though I owed him no respect or courtesy and even though I had been with other men before our marriage, I waited until our divorce was final to begin seeing any-one else. As long as a piece of paper said I was married, I respected that. Perhaps I hadn't led the most Pollyanna-perfect and respect-able life before our marriage, but deep down I was still the same decent person my parents had raised me to be, and as long as this man remained my husband by law, I was going to live up to my end of the deal, even if he never had.

Suddenly, though, I found myself single and wondering what to do. The first guy I went out with after the divorce was someone I met in an online chatroom. He was amusing and cute in a quirky sort of way, even though he was a little skinny and was a couple of years younger than I was, which I didn't usually find attractive. He was intelligent, easy to talk to, and made me laugh, and I truly, deeply needed that after all I had been through with Mr. Wrong.

We met at his apartment one Friday night to hang out. These days, folks would call it "Netflix and chill," but back then we didn't have that concept. We listened to music – Beastie Boys' "Intergalactic" was the popular song at the time, and I lost count of how many times it played that night – and it didn't take long for the alcohol to come out. What started as innocently talking and listening to music while sitting at the kitchen table shifted toward giggling antics that moved all over the house and culminated in a silliness-and-beer-fueled session of "look how we can use this sloshy waterbed as a trampoline to catapult each other across the bedroom."

So, what happens when two young, single people who are clearly attracted to each other and more than a little drunk end up staring at each other across the bed when they finally get still for a few seconds?

Yep, you guessed it. Despite my best pep talk with myself to "be good, hang out, and go home," we slept together.

After the two years I'd spent with Mr. Wrong and the countless nights of lonely sadness, tears shed over his infidelities, and so many layers of abuse and heartbreak, lying on that bed looking at an attractive, seemingly decent guy having this much fun made that do-the-right-thing pep talk fly right out the window. Combine all that heartache with a whole lot of alcohol, and I don't think I could've said, "No," even if I'd wanted to (which I really didn't).

I was beginning to like this new guy – *a lot*. I didn't know what my future was with him or if there might be one, but he said he enjoyed spending time with me, and we made plans to spend the following day together. He told me I could spend the night at his apartment since I was clearly too tipsy to drive home. I remember thinking that I should enjoy life and quit worrying all the time.

He's a nice guy who wants to get to know you.
Don't ruin it by overanalyzing and worrying.

Sometime later, the phone rang. We were silly drunk but managed to answer and talk to his roommate, Tyler, whom I had met in passing before he left the apartment to go out with his girlfriend earlier in the evening. He figured out fairly quickly how intoxicated we were as we yelled things like, "We're drunk. Why aren't you drunk?" and "Bring us more beer or don't come home!" He just laughed and hung up on us.

All I recall after that was lying down together in my newfound guy's freezing cold room, covering up with his heavy blanket, mumbling something to each other about having a fun night, giggling some more, and basically passing out. We were in that thickheaded stage of a buzz, and a sluggish feeling was settling in.

The next thing I recall was the feeling of lying on something harder than the waterbed and not knowing where I was.

"Phillip? What're you doing? Again?!" I giggled and thought this new guy of mine sure had an insatiable physical appetite. He was on top of me while I was sleeping, but I didn't feel as if I was in the waterbed, and the room was noticeably warmer, almost muggy. I still felt tipsy, the room was dark, and my head was thick.

Wait.
Where am I?

"Just say my name. Just say my name one time so I can tell him you knew it was me."

"What are you talking about, silly? I know your name. *Phillip.*" I was giggly and dizzy. The room was spinning. Reality was not quite my friend.

"Say my name. Just say it just once. Say my name so I can tell him you knew it was me. Say, 'TY-ler.' Say, 'TY-ler.' Just say my name one time. C'mon!"

Very little can snap you out of a thick-headed, semi-drunken fog faster than realizing the reason you feel as if you aren't in the comfort of the waterbed in which you fell asleep is that the guy you fell asleep next to is still in that bed while you're now in his roommate's bedroom, and the roommate is on top of you pumping away trying to get you to say his name.

My eyes flashed open. Wide open.

There was Tyler, the roommate, inside me, going at it with all he had. I was naked from the waist down, and my shirt was pushed up around my chin. I was lying on the edge of his bed with my feet on the floor while he stood over me with one knee on the bed. As drunk as I still was, I suddenly felt very alert, awake, aware.

Those are details I won't forget. *Can't forget.*

His slitty eyes. Slightly shaggy, muddy brown hair that looked as if it hadn't been washed in several days. The fact that he was shorter than Phillip. His dumpy, pasty white skin glowing in the darkness of his bedroom. The way he dragged out the "TY" in Tyler and the way he chanted it heartlessly, demandingly, harshly in my face over and over *and over* until I acknowledged him.

Neither the love and patience nor the controlling and abrupt dumping I went through with Luke had prepared me for this. The way I had been cozied and played by Will hadn't prepared me for this. The way I had been used and dismissed by Donny hadn't prepared me for this. The way I had been abused, cheated on, and abandoned by Mr. Wrong hadn't prepared me for this.

Nothing could have prepared me for this.

It is my inciting incident, the thing that changed the next 10 years of my life up to the moment I met Richard, my husband. At that moment, my life changed in ways I didn't realize and never fully understood until 18 years later when I finally stopped running from my story and listened to what "God was trying to tell me."

My inciting incident made things fall apart in August 1998. It took years for me to let things fall back together. I had to admit it and allow it. I had to own it in the midst of being so powerfully good at avoiding it. Through all these years, though, I have known this is my story to tell.

Sadly, it isn't my only story. It is my falling-apart moment. I spent the next 18 years tormented in so many ways, but I now understand how so many of those ways can be traced to the moment when "TY-ler" was on top of me with those slitty eyes in that dark room as I lay on that hard bed hearing his harshly whispered demands that I say his name.

You can bet my eyes were wide open. They may not have been before, but they sure were then. Suddenly, about so many things, and from then on.

"Tyler?"

"See? I knew you knew it was me all along. Good girl." With that said, he leaned closer. I could feel his breath on the side of my face.

I stared at the ceiling.

"Tyler," I whispered. "TY-ler. *Not* Phillip."

He pulled away, grinned, leaned back in and let that shaggy hair brush against my face as he continued his business on top of me.

I never fought back.

I didn't scream, not even on the inside. I didn't say another word or feel anything. I was in shock. You always think if you find your-self in a situation like that, you'll come up fighting, kicking, and clawing like a wild animal to get away. I thought that, too, but when given the opportunity, I didn't.

I did nothing.

I lay there as if I were in a coma. All I could do was wonder what would happen to my relationship with Phillip. Never once did it occur to me to go to the hospital to be tested for sexually transmitted diseases, to report I had been assaulted, or to worry what this experi-ence was doing to me mentally, physically, emotionally, spiritually.

As ridiculous as it sounds now, I didn't think of myself as a vic-tim. I was a woman who allowed myself into a bad situation that I *chose* to put myself in. The result was that I let something happen to me. I didn't fight back, so if I were to tell anyone what happened, it wouldn't matter. I knew enough about how these stories end to know that, by being drunk, by allowing the vulnerability, by going into the room with him (whether I was in my right mind or not), and by not fighting back, I would be told it was my choice to let it happen.

In my mind, assault – and Heaven forbid I consider using the word "rape" – happened in dark alleys where women were attacked by nameless, faceless men. Trips to the hospital, police reports, court dates, counselors, and years of healing were involved.

This was not *that*.

It was nothing more than a drunken night that primarily involved my needing to have known better. It was a thick-headed, shouldn't-have-been-there-in-the-first-place moment that I had no one to blame for but myself. The wisdom that comes with 18 years of time to think on what happened, with age, with experience, and with a clear head that isn't clouded by alcohol is that I know now I should have fought back – kicked, hit, screamed, done whatever I could to get him off me – and I should have gone immediately to the hospital to be examined and to report the crime.

But I didn't.

I was paralyzed by shame, fear, and uncertainty. The dizziness and thick-headedness from being drunk had begun to pass, and as drunk and unaware as I had been before, I was suddenly every bit as alert and stingingly on edge since Tyler had finished and moved to the other side of the room.

I had no idea where most of my clothes were; I was wearing only my shirt. I was the definition of exposed and vulnerable lying there on the edge of the bed not sure what to do or where to go. I assumed the rest of my clothes were still on Phillip's bedroom floor, but I wasn't even sure what direction that might be from where I was. I sat up on the edge of the bed and tried to cover myself, perching there as if I needed his permission to move from that spot.

"You know I have to tell Phillip."

The look of contempt on Tyler's face challenged me to go wake Phillip up right then and tell him anything I wanted him to know. I remember lots of exact things that were said that night because I couldn't possibly forget them if I tried, but at that moment, I was in a daze. I don't recall everything he said in word-for-word detail because my brain's inner monologue was rattling off its own thoughts at a whirlwind pace at the same time Tyler was lecturing me about the finer points of why it wouldn't do any good for me to tell anyone what happened between us.

It went something to the effect of how Phillip would be mad at both of us, I had wanted it just as badly as he did when he came in Phillip's bedroom to get me, I had stumbled in there without being carried so it must've been my own free will, and I knew it was him all along and was teasing him or I wouldn't have said his name.

When he said that, my feet found their energy, and suddenly that lack of permission to move didn't feel as if it were freezing me to that spot. I bolted from the room, found my way down the hall to Phillip's room, and gathered my clothes as quietly as I could. I don't recall blinking or breathing or hearing my heart beat a single thump as I hurriedly dressed in a blur of fighting back tears and nausea. The sun was almost up, and Phillip was still passed out face down in the waterbed with his arm stretched across to where I had been lying beside him. For all he knew, I was still there snuggled in and ready to wake up and start the day, a day we had planned to spend having fun together.

The drive home was a blur. I left my clothes just inside the door and went straight to a shower so hot it felt like I was trying to purge his touch from my skin. I washed my hair, scrubbed my face, brushed my teeth, and stood in the shower letting the scorching water pour straight down over my head. Despite my anxiety and uncertainty about what had happened, l didn't think of myself as a victim. Words like "slut" and "idiot" echoed in my thoughts all day. I beat myself up for doing this to my potential with Phillip before it had a chance to grow. I questioned whether I should tell him, but I owed it to both of us to start off whatever was between us on the right foot.

So, I picked up the phone and called him. As much as I wanted to pretend nothing happened, I knew telling him was the right thing to do. Thankfully, Phillip answered the phone. I'm not sure what I would've done or said or felt if Tyler had answered. For all I know, I would've gone into shock and simply sat on the phone in silence listening to that familiar sound of his breathing in my ear. It was Phillip on the phone, though, and he wanted to know why I left without saying goodbye. There was a slight defensiveness in his voice.

Does he think I ditched out because I don't like him
or does he already know what happened?

How am I supposed to tell him
I had sex with his best friend
while he was sleeping soundly in the next room
with the belief that I was lying next to him under his arm
basking in the glow of whatever this new relationship is?

I didn't tell him Tyler assaulted me. It simply wasn't within my brain's muddled capabilities. Instead, I told him what I saw as the truth – that when Tyler got home, he came into the room where we were sleeping, that I was still drunk and went in the next room with him without realizing what I was doing, and that we slept together. I told him it was a mistake I regretted, that I would take it back if I could, and that I was sorry.

His reaction was mostly disgust and was slightly underwhelming compared with what I expected. After living with Mr. Wrong's emotional abuse and mental warfare, I expected Phillip to fight back, to blow up, to blame me, to tell me what a terrible, no-good, dreadfully horrible mistake of a potential girlfriend I was and how this ruined what could've been something great.

He didn't. His reaction was borderline subdued. He scoffed at me and said he shouldn't be surprised and indicated this wasn't the first time he had encountered a woman he couldn't trust. From what he said, it seemed as if he had experienced something almost identical to this before. He said his support was with Tyler and not me, and the conversation ended. After hanging up the phone, I over-analyzed his reaction.

Have I been played?
Is this some sort of cat-and-mouse game between them
with girls they bring home?
Start with one roommate. End up with the other.
No long-term strings attached for either one,
and they both get what they want.
The girl ends up with nothing but questions,
confusion, and embarrassment.

Paranoia began to set in. Was I part of a sick game between Phillip and Tyler? A couple of hours later, Tyler called. He wanted to come over and talk. He told me Phillip had confronted him and things hadn't gone well. He wanted to apologize to both of us and make things right, but he felt he had to start with me to make that happen. He wanted to see if we could set things right between us.

I needed to believe him and wanted so desperately to set my world back on its straight-and-narrow path. After all I'd been through with Mr. Wrong in the two years before that and all that had happened with Phillip and Tyler, I needed something to go right. The formerly naïve girl with the now wide-open eyes who still wanted the world to be a place filled with good people simply replied, against her better judgment, but with as much hope as she could muster, "Okay. Come over."

When he showed up that night, he was surprisingly respectful. He kept his distance. He was polite. We talked. Discussion of the night before didn't immediately come up in conversation.

We talked about television and movies, which provided no common ground between my love of quirky comedies and his appreciation of action films. We discussed what we did for a living. Despite there being only a couple of years' age difference between us, I had a master's degree and a career in marketing and public relations, while he was a junior college student unsure of what he wanted to do with no real concern about it. Thirty minutes or so passed while we mindlessly, awkwardly chatted. He seemed nice enough, not particularly interesting or my type, but a mostly tolerable guy. Under different circumstances, I might have wanted to set him up with one of my friends.

I hadn't allowed him into my home to become better acquainted, though. My goal had been to, as he put it, "set things right" and talk through what happened, so I brought up the night before out of the blue as he talked. He saw it as an opening to move closer to me on the couch, as if we somehow needed to talk quietly about this particular topic.

"I thought you wanted to be with me," he told me, appearing quite sincere as he gazed at me through all that shaggy hair hanging around those slitty eyes.

He tried to take my hand. I jerked it away.

I assured him I had not wanted to be with him. I had been there to hang out with Phillip, his roommate and supposedly best friend, and I was not the type of girl to sleep with two men in one night, although I realized he couldn't have known that. In fact, I really didn't want to be the type of girl who went out with someone, got drunk on the first date, and slept with him, but if that were to happen, I certainly would not want to leave myself open to having something like *this* happen.

He said I seemed sweet and that he could tell I was upset. He told me Phillip was threatening to kick him out and had said he was done with me and any future we had together. He said it had been a rough day at the apartment and that he was sorry all this had happened.

All I could hear in what he said was the pulsing of my own disappointment that hung around the words "any future we had together." When Tyler said Phillip was done with me and any possible future together, I took a verbal punch in the gut that made me miss what he said for the next minute or so. He could tell what he said had that effect on me, and our efforts to set things straight began to turn into a support group meeting. He tried to win my sympathy, telling me how he and Phillip had been friends for several years and how he couldn't believe this was tearing them apart.

As difficult as it is for me to understand now looking back, I actually began feeling sorry for him. At the time, I refused to see myself as a victim, so it wasn't a difficult jump for me to see myself as the disgraceful whore who shattered the enduring bond of two best friends. In the back of my mind, I was clinging to humiliation and regret, but in the forefront, I was thinking, "This guy is devastated by the loss of his friend. What can I do to help?" My caretaker side kicked in, and I found myself comforting and reassuring my attacker.

Yep. Let that sink in.

The mind of a person dealing with something like sexual assault is an unpredictable thing. I sat in my own home on my own couch less than 24 hours after this man knowingly took advantage of me while I was incapacitated consoling him about the fact that he might have lost his best friend because of *me.*

To this day, I cannot comprehend the depths of irrationality involved in that decision, but I know I wanted my life back. I wanted an exit of the drama and heartache and people with ulterior motives and malicious intent from my life, so if that meant shoving aside rationality, buying into the ridiculousness he was feeding me, and forgetting the shame and horror of the night before, then so be it.

I was not prepared for what came next, though.

"Maybe you and I could make a go of it," he said.

My world, my brain, my heart, what little composure was left stopped turning. I felt as if I was lying on that hard bed in that dark, muggy room once again staring at the ceiling trying to figure out what was going on.

Did he really just say he and I should explore a
relationship?
What is happening right now?

Once again, he reached for my hand, but, this time, I didn't instantly jerk away. It pained me to let him touch me, but it also felt nice that someone wanted to. I had experienced far too many negative things in that house while married to Mr. Wrong, and very rarely had anyone spoken kindly or shown interest in me. I certainly didn't want it to be Tyler, but I had already lost Phillip.

What if I did want to go in his room with him?
What if he came into Phillip's room and I hit on him?
Maybe I initiated the whole thing.
I was so drunk.
I shouldn't have been there with a guy I didn't know.
Clearly, he didn't pick me up and carry me.
I had to get up and walk in there on my own.
Maybe I did want to be with him.

So many thoughts churned through my mind. Confusion was the order of the moment. I wanted stability, peace, love. Phillip was lost to me. Tyler was right beside me, and clearly, I was the one at fault for the entire incident, regardless of what part he played. Maybe this was my chance to salvage some small piece of my dignity. If I gave him a chance, he might be a decent guy.

He continued holding my hand, a little more firmly and then with both hands, moving in a little more closely as he did. I didn't want to move closer to him, but I didn't resist as he advanced. I don't know why. At this stage in life, I look back and think so many things.

Get up! Run! Yell!
You didn't want that.
Why didn't you say something?
Why were you such an idiot?

Why did you sit there as if you were frozen,
as if you didn't have a choice?
You always have a choice!
Why didn't you stop this from happening again?!
You didn't want this!

But I didn't stop it. His advances were like a drug, and I was the whore addict who needed her fix of love and attention. I stopped talking and walked behind him like a zombie while he held both my hands – firmly and with purpose – and led me to my bedroom. I let him take off my clothes, forcing an awkward smile as if I were shy or maybe just unsure when I was really thinking what a horrible mistake this was. I uncomfortably played along but mostly lay there like a robot doing what I was told for the short time it took for him to be done.

Afterwards, I asked if he was serious about trying to make a go of it. I didn't really want that, but we had just slept together. He had taken the time to come to my home, to talk to me, to share his feelings about his friend. He slept with me when I wasn't drunk this time, so he was interested in me on some level, and I had allowed him to be there, even if I felt trapped in an unfortunate out-of-body experience the whole time. I watched him getting dressed and thought he wasn't that bad looking and that maybe if we spent time together, I would eventually want to know him.

Through the humiliation and shock that still held a grip on me from the night before, I could hear my brain starting to rationalize and telling me to make the best of a bad situation, despite the fact that I felt nauseous every time he spoke, especially when his words were in lower tones that reminded me of his harsh whisper that continuously pierced the darkness as he insisted I say his name.

For the second time in 24 hours, I found myself sitting on the edge of a bed with more questions than answers while this man stood before me getting dressed. Everything around me moved painfully slowly, but inside my body, everything – my mind, heartbeat, breathing, sense of direction, feelings, pretty much everything that could be anything – was on fast forward.

I am so lost right now.
I don't know who I am or how
I got to this point in my life
or what I'm thinking or doing or seeing
or why I'm making the decisions I'm making.

I don't know what I would've done if he had said he wanted to explore a relationship. If he had turned to me and pledged his undying love or tried to kiss me or hold my hand and talk to me sweetly or even sat down next to me on the bed, would I have recoiled in shock? Or would I have sunk into his arms and been thankful that someone reached out to me with tenderness and wanted to be wanted in that way so badly that I bought into it regardless of how disingenuous it felt?

Those moments happen only on the big screen. In reality, the bad guy never turns out to be the chivalrous prince who loves unconditionally and sweeps you off your feet with the right words at the right time to save your day and mend your heart. Instead of resurrecting my brain from its flatlined fog with tender words and some sort of romantic gesture after our time together, he nonchalantly continued getting dressed and shrugged his shoulders.

"Are you going to try to work things out with Phillip? Are you going to tell him you came over here to see me?"

He politely smirked. Politely, but a slight smirk, nonetheless.

"This was fun. Maybe we can do it again some time," he said with a quiet, dismissive softness in his voice as he approached the door. "I'll call you."

And just like that, he was gone.

I fell back on the bed and stared at the ceiling as the door closed behind him. In the quiet, lonely stillness around me, I could hear Will's voice at the top of my stairs three years earlier with the same hollow promise. When Will spoke those words, I swooned a little with joy and overwhelming innocence as I watched him stroll away and naïvely wondered how long it would be before he made good on his promise. This time when I heard those words, I found myself hoping and praying with the same depth of sincerity, earnestness, and wholehearted honesty in such a wretchedly sad way that the promise would, in fact, never come true.

Thankfully, it didn't. That was the last time I laid eyes on Tyler or heard his voice, at least outside my mind. I still hear it at least once a day, sometimes more, demanding I say his name, "just once so I can tell him you knew it was me." I long ago accepted that his voice is part of my life, no matter how much time passes and no matter how much old wounds try to heal.

Chapter Six

Wandering

It's impossible to describe to someone who hasn't lived through a sexual assault the thoughts that went through my mind as I lay there silently numb and didn't fight back, how I felt when I snapped out of a drunken fog with someone on top of me demanding I say his name, and why I allowed myself to sleep with him again even though I obviously didn't want to.

I truly wish I could explain.

For years and years and even now, I have prayed for any small shadow of reasoning somewhere in my actions. It didn't make sense to me as it was happening, and it still doesn't make sense to me after years of self-examination and time to heal.

Our brains are powerfully sharp tools equipped with the ability to either guide us through hazardous terrain with razor-sharp accuracy or to send us hurtling down the side of Mental Mountain hitting every jagged memory's edge. When that burdensome Mr. Bear plops cripplingly on our chests to remind us of the pain, our brains either protect us by sending him away without a moment's hesitation or decorate for a welcome home party and set up a cozy corner where he can hibernate.

Every person who goes through such trauma rejoins the functioning world differently. For some, inner strength emerges like a suit of armor. These fighters each take unique paths, but their common bond is how they warrior through recovery, never letting what happened define them.

I heard a remarkably empowering quote once from Carl Gustav Jung that simply states, "I am not what happened to me. I am what I choose to become." How simple yet powerful and appropriate for our survivor friends who leap resolutely into their full coat of inner strength and soldier through. It doesn't mean they're okay with what happened, and it also doesn't mean they're okay with talking about it freely or being reminded of the assault. Similarly, it also doesn't mean they *don't* want to talk about it or that they're going to pretend it never happened. It simply means they made their peace and choose to move on with life in a positive way, sometimes helping others, sometimes simply helping themselves. Whatever the path, they choose strength.

For others, withdrawing into themselves and never speaking of the assault seems like the best option. This was my path. For a long time, I didn't leave my house other than to go to work. I needed time to be with just myself, whoever that was anymore, and to focus on repairing my brokenness.

Each day, I left home just in time to get to work and returned as soon as the workday ended to retreat behind locked doors and ignore the world spinning along without me. It became increasingly difficult to ignore Mr. Wrong's patrolling in the evenings, but I tried to stay in the back of the house and pretend I didn't hear him revving his engine every time he drove by to let me know he was watching.

Rather than get away from the house to bond with nearly forgotten friends or rejoin my church, go to movies or restaurants, find a hobby or do something centering and constructive to help the healing process, I withdrew into an online world that did nothing to promote recovery from pains that seemed to hang palpably around me like accessories for my clothing and decorations for my home. Most nights found me sitting in my back room at the computer talking in chat rooms. Fake online friends were far easier to manage than face-to-face interactions. Online, I could be anyone I wanted to be, and most of my real-life friends were long gone by that point thanks to Mr. Wrong's isolation games and my own shame.

Chatting online was a controlled environment where I called the shots and could be anyone and say anything without fear of retribution. If someone didn't like what I said, I simply left the room or blocked them. We never had to work out our differences or see each other again. It was the ultimate chance to withdraw into a world where no one controlled me. I regularly chatted online until 1 or 2 a.m. and found myself having animated conversations with people I had never met from both far away and right down the road and, most importantly, smiling and laughing for the first time in longer than I could recall.

It didn't take long to start talking and flirting with men online. That's sort of the nature of chat rooms. As much as people say they're innocently online to talk and make friends (and I suppose some genuinely are), discussions in chat rooms take a personal turn quite quickly. It was nothing for me to have four or five chat sessions going at once on any given night. It was a non-heartbreaking way to receive attention and feel good about myself, regardless of how artificial, temporary, and hollow it might be.

Life was a blur. My heart was broken from the abandonment I had experienced with Luke, from the abuse I went through with Mr. Wrong, and from the worthlessness and shame I felt after Tyler. Talking to men online made me feel on top of the world. They treated me as if I were amazing. They laughed at my jokes. They thought I was adorable. They didn't care that I wasn't the prettiest or thinnest girl or that I didn't have the nicest house in town. They didn't need to hear about the guy who decided not to marry me after all I went through to be with him or my cheating ex-husband or the fact that I super-failed my first attempt at a date after my divorce.

They asked how my day was, how I planned to spend the weekend, what I liked to do for fun, my favorite color, food, music, movie, where I went to college, and what I liked to watch on TV. We exchanged pictures, and I accepted that just as my picture wasn't always current, their pictures probably weren't either. At least the pictures gave us an idea of who we were at some point.

In the cyber world, most people were promoting a slicked-up, thinned-down, glossed-over version of themselves, and that was okay with me. More often than not, the conversations meandered aimlessly once or twice at a light and chatty pace with mild flirting before we never spoke again. Occasionally, though, there was someone who hung around, and phone numbers might be exchanged.

If the conversation reached that point, I admitted my picture was old and that I had gained weight and didn't quite look like the picture I sent. I apologized and said if I'd known we were going to meet, I would've sent a more accurate picture and that I understood if he didn't want to talk anymore. Surprisingly, I recall only one time that revelation was a problem.

Against my better judgment, I met a few of these online "friends" in real life. At that low point in life, the attention felt well worth the risk. Being desired and needed and valued was all I wanted, and even if it lasted only a couple of hours while we got to know each other, that was all I needed to revive my spark and remind myself what a smile felt like, however hollow it may actually have been.

In the midst of these chat sessions, I met a nice man from a town several hours away with whom I spent more time talking than anyone else. We connected over the phone and spent countless hours talking and laughing nearly every night. He drove in one weekend to accompany me to a wedding four weeks to the day after the incident with Tyler. I was a nervous wreck at the thought of actual human interaction, especially wondering how Mr. Wrong would react if he drove by and saw a car he didn't recognize in the driveway.

My friend was nice, handsome, witty, intelligent, and treated me like a lady, something to which I was no longer accustomed and quite undeserving, at least in my mind. We spent a wonderfully comfortable weekend together talking, laughing, watching football, and cooking before he revealed he was still occasionally talking to his ex-girlfriend and needed to figure out what was going on with that relationship before venturing into something new. Despite the many times we had discussed how perfect we were for each other and the extra night he stayed, not wanting to go home and end our time together, I didn't fight for a chance to be with him. I let him drive away the next morning back to his hometown, back to his ex-girlfriend, and out of my life.

We had everything in common two people could possibly share, but there was no sense in asking him to pursue anything long dis-tance when he had up-close-and-personal issues to resolve with someone else. I had invested what little emotional energy I could muster in getting to know him and trust him, and when things ended relatively quickly, I was stick-a-fork-in-me *done*. I couldn't balance my need for him to choose me over his ex-girlfriend with my brain's telling me there was no reason for him to pick me when she was clearly the better choice.

Why would he want you?
What guy would want someone like you who shows up
for a date with one guy and ends up sleeping with him
and his roommate and then sleeps with the roommate
again the next night, too?
He's a really nice guy.
Let him drive away. Let him go back to his life.
Ruin your own life and leave his alone.

So, I didn't speak up and say what I wanted to say. I didn't fight for him. I let him leave wishing I had asked him to choose me but believing he wouldn't think I was worth the effort. How could I expect anyone else to see me as worthwhile when I didn't see myself that way?

However, meeting this man boosted my confidence and made me realize there were decent men online and that the idea they were all predators who would kidnap me and bury me in a field if I were to meet them in real life was inane, even though that's what my coworkers tried to tell me was surely going to happen. They had no understanding of how many people I talked to daily or how many I had the potential to meet if I wanted to.

Hurting from what I saw as the loss of a great guy who deserved better than me and accepting the fact that I wouldn't soon feel differently, I numbly, blindly, haphazardly plodded through connections for brief moments with men, but never once did I feel anything approaching love or intimacy. I discovered that sex was power and that I could wield that power like a mighty sword. I used men. I let them use me. Sex was about power or it was about bargaining or it was about making someone love me, but it was never about love. It was never something I enjoyed or was swept away by or let myself give in to fully or even in some small way. Sex had been used as power over me, and, in some bizarre way, I was attempting to harness that power and control it so it could never be used against me again, even though I never consciously processed that as my intention until many years later.

Coming out of a drunken fog with someone I had met only in passing on top of me had stolen that. I didn't realize it at the time. I never consciously resented Tyler or mourned what happened. I never cried. Not once. I didn't become bitter toward men or live in fear.

It didn't matter how far I strayed from the morals with which I had been brought up. In fact, the further I could run from them, the better. I needed to feel like a different person, to slip into a sort of alter ego who controlled my decisions and had the power to tell the former good girl who let herself be stepped on to shut up, sit down, and let this far more dominating person direct the show.

Any time I talked to someone new online, the façade came up. The huntress was after her prey with the goal of winning affection and attention. Even if nothing came of it off-screen in the real world (and most of the time, nothing did), I wanted them to want me.

They *had* to want me.

To me, I was nobody. To everyone else, I wanted to be the world, and I was someone different to each person. Online, I was an all-around-just-right, all-American girl next door loved by all – the advice giver, the funny girl, the flirt, the sweetheart, much like the woman I wished I could be in real life. At work, I had a professional job that didn't require me to socialize after hours. As far as my coworkers knew, I was recently divorced from a not-so-great marriage and turning my attention to rebuilding and meeting new people. They heard me talk about going out occasionally, but they never had a reason to meet anyone in my personal life.

My family lived two states away, and the only things they ever knew of my day-to-day life were the flowery pictures I painted for them on the telephone. They believed I was piecing life back together after going through financial stress, dealing with purging Mr. Wrong from my life, and meeting new friends, all ideas that sounded good to them after the dark days through which I'd recently trudged.

I didn't have to worry what my friends thought. I'd lost most of them when I got married, and my new life was so foreign to them that attempting to reconnect wasn't worth the painful effort it inevitably took. The few friends I'd made while married to Mr. Wrong still popped in and out of my life, but they had their own lives to live, and I was moving pretty quickly in directions that didn't include them.

My life spiraled endlessly through the online world for several months. I attached myself to a chat room frequented by people who lived in or around my area and found myself feeling like chat royalty when I emerged as one of the room's leaders. When I entered the room each night, multiple chatters cheerfully greeted me by my real name rather than my screenname or called me by one of the clever nicknames we all had for each other, and my private messages lit up the second I signed on. Online chat soon evolved into real-world get-togethers, and I replaced my old friends with these new friends who felt as if they'd been comfortably in my life for years.

Every day, I came home from work, put something together for dinner as quickly as possible if I hadn't already picked up something on the way home and took the plate to the desk in my spare bedroom where my computer was set up so I could sit well into the night chatting as fast as my fingers could type, sometimes with phone, private messages, and chat room conversations all going at the same time. There were even times all three types of conversations were with the same person at the same time about different topics. During my growing obsession with the online world and the following of people my friends and I had collected who thought we were interesting and who gave me the unconditional attention I craved, I met Jeff, a man who lived a couple of hours away and had custody of his son. A ready-made family of two guys to love and tend to? That seemed like the normal life I wanted custom-made just for me, and he was a straight-shooting, blue-collar type who made me feel important. He was decent looking and funny, and he had an unpredictable, edgy side and several tattoos, which made the formerly mild-mannered, quietly obedient, modest Southern girl in me swoon a little at the very thought of how "bad" he must surely be.

"I've always wanted a tattoo," I told him.

"So why don't you have one?" he asked.

I didn't have one because I'd always been led to believe tattoos were trashy and only low-class people had them, especially if you were a woman. Deep down, I didn't believe that to be true and had always secretly wanted one but had, as usual, let my fear of what people might think get in the way of what I wanted.

"I don't know. I just never got up the courage and never had anyone in my life who knew about tattoos and could go with me."

"Well, you have me, and I have several," he said. "You'll come here this weekend and get one."

It never occurred to me to tell him "No." I was already swept up in his charm. So, just as he said I should do, a few days later I drove up to where he and his son lived and got my first tattoo. I spent a fun, cozy weekend with Jeff and his son and got to meet his mother. That weekend launched yet another dysfunctional relationship that saw us through a year and a half of an on-again, off-again roller coaster that brought with it a river's worth of tears and frustration, living together after we'd already decided not to see each other anymore (supposedly just as roommates, although that didn't last), and the one constant between us – the fact that we didn't know how to stay away from each other.

During one of our off-again phases, I developed a no-strings-attached relationship with Tony, a divorced father of three who lived about 30 minutes away. Tony had started out as an online friend who came to our monthly chat room parties but was slowly becoming more. With Jeff mostly out of my life for the moment, Tony had stepped into the hole Jeff left behind and filled the space quite nicely. He was a kinder, less challenging version of Jeff who was much happier doing low-key things, and I needed that energy after the last time Jeff and I had parted ways.

A few weeks into my getting to know Tony, Jeff came into town for one of our chat room parties and asked if he and a friend could stay with me for the night. His son was staying the weekend with his mother, and it seemed like enough time had passed that it might be fun to reconnect. Tony knew my history with Jeff and knew we had remained friends no matter what else we had ever been. He assured me he was okay with having the guys stay at my apartment, and since Tony and I weren't serious (and he was still talking through a mountain of issues with his ex-girlfriend), telling him they were staying with me was really more of a courtesy.

Tony and I spent a fun day together before the party, and he had already left to go back to his apartment when Jeff and his friend arrived. The party was in Tony's town, so we went straight to his apartment so I could introduce them. Jeff and Tony instantly hit it off and were practically inseparable.

As we often did in those days, we drank throughout the night. When we were getting ready to leave, I saw Jeff and Tony high-five. Tony reached out, took my hand, and spun me toward Jeff, who held a firm grasp on my hand as we began walking toward the door to leave.

"What just happened?" I asked.

"I tagged in my buddy," Tony laughed. "Tag! You're it!"

He and Jeff slapped their hands together in a high-five once again and spun me around from one to the other back and forth, laughing. Earlier, I'd wondered why they were talking so closely and grinning at me. They talked so much when they met about so many things that it hadn't occurred to me I might be one of the topics of conversation.

In my awkwardly semi-drunken state, I laughed right along with them. I didn't know what else to do, and saying I was embarrassed would've only made them act out more. Jeff had my keys, and I knew him well enough to know he would've driven off in my car leaving me there to figure out how to get home if I'd argued with him, so I said nothing. He held tightly to my hand and nearly dragged me to the car with a smirking grin as I followed along in silence.

He had drunk a couple of beers here and there throughout the night and smoked weed earlier in the evening. Thankfully, he was sober now and able to drive us back to Tony's house to drop him off. Even though I said I wasn't going to drink, I'd been offered one drink after another by either Tony or Jeff most of the night, which, looking back later, didn't seem like a coincidence. Getting driven home this way wasn't my first choice, but getting left behind still somewhat inebriated as my own car drove away without me didn't seem like much of an option either.

With a couple of girls from the bar tagging along in their own car behind us, Tony didn't waste time going inside when we got to his place. I stumbled around outside, starting to sober up but still somewhat drunk and unsure of why we were still there. Jeff was walking around, too, calling the name of one of the girls who followed us. I walked around the back of the apartments to tell him he was wasting his time.

"She went in with Tony."

"She did what?!" he yelled. As he stomped his frustrations out around the yard and made obscene gestures at Tony's apartment, he was going on about how she was supposed to sneak away from her friends and meet him out back.

"You were going to make out with *that* girl?" I asked.

He stopped, turned to stare at me, and let out the loudest, sneering laugh. His next words pretty well shocked me out of caring one way or the other what he had planned with her or how angry or frustrated he was.

"*You're* here," he sneered.

Without another word, he took my hand firmly once again, just as he had at the club, and pulled me through the dark yard behind Tony's apartment. When we reached the back corner, he abruptly pushed me against the fence, kissing me, running his hands under my clothes and all over me.

I tried to tell myself he was spontaneous and passionate, but I knew better. It didn't matter to him that it was me, that we had more than a year's history together, that we had shared better moments than this. I was "here," even if I wasn't the woman he'd planned to meet, and he didn't care who he had against that fence or against his body.

Without warning, he stopped kissing and groping me, grabbed my arm, spun me quickly toward the fence, and jerked my pants down. He knew I still held firmly to fairly deep feelings for him, and when he had kissed me earlier in the evening at the party, I hadn't stopped him, so it wasn't beyond the realm of possibility that he might've pursued more later in the evening.

But in Tony's back yard?
Pressed against the fence?
Just because I was "here"?

I didn't know what to say or do. My pants were around my ankles. I was holding on to the fence mostly to keep my face from getting slammed into it. A couple of times I tried to straighten my back, but his firmly insistent hand pushed me back down and kept me bent over where he wanted me. I took it all in silence looking through the holes in the chain link and staring beyond at the stars in the sky for the two minutes or so it took for him to be done. I was partially drunk, still mentally attached, and heartbroken.

Is this one of those weird, wild stories
you tell your girlfriends
and giggle about the craziness of over drinks,
or is this something bad that's happening to me?
I really don't know.

It was Jeff, and Jeff was unpredictable and uninhibited. I had learned to go with it long before this moment. I didn't like being "here," but I liked Jeff, or at least I thought I did, and he was going home with me later and not with someone else. On some level at that increasingly detached stage in life, it simply felt good to be someone's choice, even if I couldn't be his first.

Most days, I felt overweight, unwanted, and lonely nearly every second of every hour when I wasn't sitting in front of the computer feeling like an online rock star. This moment, however awkward and shameful it was, made me feel swept away, different, and dangerous on some deep-down, dig-below-the-grossness level, even if I had to sugarcoat it and talk myself into believing it when he was done.

Even if I had to rationalize it to myself. At least I felt something, unlike most of the time when I only felt numb.

That didn't make it okay. Of course, it didn't. *It was wrong.*

I knew it *then,* and I know it *now.* I didn't want to be treated that way or chosen simply because I was "here." I didn't want to be shoved against a fence staring through the holes at the moon and stars wondering if God ever saw the things I got myself into, and I would never want to be abandoned in the yard to pull myself together and eventually find my way to the car when it was over. Jeff saw it as reckless and exciting, one of those stories we could look back on as part of our youthful Glory Days, and he would have laughed in my face if I told him how violated, demeaned, and taken advantage of I felt.

Looking back, it breaks my heart to think that I allowed him to do that to me without fighting or screaming in his smug face.

No. You won't treat me this way.
You will not pass me off by tagging yourself in.
You will not choose me simply because I'm here.
You will want me because I'm worth spending time with,
and if you ever earn me as your own,
you will be glad I'm yours.
You'll joyfully spend the rest of your life
doing whatever you can to keep me.
I'm not a piece of skin wrapped around a hole
that you can stick something in whenever
you feel the need for gratification.

*I'm a person with feelings, even if I don't know
how to feel them anymore.
But I will someday, and when I do, I will erase you
and your kind from my life forever.*

And that's what I did. Eventually.

It took many years and the process of writing this book, finding my way back to a more centered faith in a Higher Power, and gaining perspective on what's important in life, but that's exactly what I did. I finally realized it really is okay to be okay and to not allow old demons left behind by bad choices and bad people to haunt me. I wish I had achieved that centered, happier-with-myself, able-to-say-no place sooner, but I was still running away from what I knew I was supposed to do.

Unfortunately, I went through seven more rough years after that night against the fence with Jeff before life began to even out, and it was another 10 years after that before I began writing this book and sifting through the mental and emotional damage I didn't even realize needed to be untangled inside me.

"Sex had been used as power over me, and, in
some bizarre way, I was attempting to harness that
power and control it so it could never be used
against me again, even though I never consciously
processed that as my intention
until many years later."

Chapter Seven

Permission to be Done

Sometimes when you're as done and over life and relationships as I was, you make a dumb decision that seems like the right thing at the time. I seem to have a knack for making them in long, ongoing series.

After I finally stopped seeing Jeff, I met who I thought was a safe-choice military man and got engaged. Two weeks before the wedding, while he was on a deployment to Korea, I joined Jeff and his son at his mom's house for the weekend. We felt as if we owed it to each other to part ways with some sort of closure on the relationship.

Of course, it wasn't long before old feelings reared their dysfunctional heads. My engagement ring went into my purse, and we were soon holding hands. His mom was proclaiming to all who would listen that we were true loves destined to be together no matter how much we tried to fight it. The second night, we had a long-overdue, lay-it-all-on-the-table talk, and rational thought prevailed.

He gave me his blessing and told me I needed to get married without looking back.

"If I have to," he said, "I'll come to the wedding and make sure you say 'I do.'"

I told him if he showed up, there wouldn't be a wedding because I'd probably run back up the aisle. We both laughed, but his next words assured me we were done.

"I won't let you. You *need* to marry this guy."

The look on his face told me all I needed to know. He was letting me go once and for all. Even though I was glancing over my shoulder now and then to see if Jeff came bursting through the church doors, I married my military man two weeks later without incident. We moved to Ft. Benning, Georgia, where I promptly wished I had run back up the aisle whether Jeff was there or not after discovering I had once again saddled myself to a ride for which I was grossly unprepared.

The man I thought was a mildly mannered, safe choice from a respectably good family announced out of the blue to me as we were about 30 minutes into the drive toward our honeymoon trip that he hoped we would "eventually progress to a point in our marriage where we can have an open relationship." The more he talked about his past and the things he wanted for our life together, the more I realized this was not the life for which I had prayed or thought I'd entered when I said, "I do."

By that point, though, we were married. I refused to give up. He seemed like a decent guy who could be reasoned with, and he had a great sense of humor. We got along well most of the time, and we were each other's best friends, as a married couple should be. I adored my stepchild and in-laws, and I became quite close with his grandmother, who reminded me so much of my own who had been gone since I was 15. I was determined to make the best of it by working through whatever issues arose. As long as he wasn't cheating or treating me like Mr. Wrong had, I was sure we could work through whatever disagreements came our way.

Five years into our marriage, he was out of the military, and we were back living near my family. Our friendship was still fairly strong most of the time, but we weren't good at the fundamentals of being a husband and wife and disagreed on things such as faith and parenting. I had lost a significant amount of weight to improve my health (which worked) and our marriage (which didn't work). Owning our first home was piling on new levels of stress, and we were going through difficult stages in our careers. We were spending more time apart than together, and being married seemed more of a practical solution to living than a choice to spend our lives together. When we were together, we weren't. He retreated to his part of the house. I stayed in mine. Physical contact was practically non-existent. If I pushed the idea of being together physically, he went to the computer to look up sex-related things to get in the mood. Much to my embarrassment as his wife who was right there in front of him and begging for attention in the real world, his online habit was something he indulged in quite often.

We were mostly friendly roommates who occasionally argued about ridiculous things, shared expenses, and happened to sleep in the same bed. End of story. As usual, no one from the outside look-ing in would have known our marriage was anything but solid. My habit of compartmentalizing is matched only by my ability to put up a good front for the world to see.

Smile.
Keep dancing.
Don't let the world see what happens
when the curtain closes at the show's finale.
Never let them see the face under the makeup
after the smile gets wiped off
as the last note fades from the music.

I was more miserable than I let my family and friends see or that I even admitted to myself. Thinking of being miserable with a man who was basically a decent person to me for the most part felt selfish. He had his flaws, but he was not an inherently bad person. He didn't cheat. He didn't yell at me. He didn't throw things. He was home at night when I went to bed. He went places with me and didn't act embarrassed. He was just as much by my side when I was overweight as when I lost weight. He came from a good fam-ily. He had given me a stepchild who was like my own biological child.

Still, though, there were red flags. There were things that made me think, "This isn't right." As usual, I was red flag colorblind.

Around this time, we began socializing with an alcohol-driven, rules-are-made-to-be-broken group. Unfortunately, that placed us right where he had always wanted us to be as a couple – with plenty of opportunities to find people to bring into our marriage.

With my weight loss came newfound confidence and improved health, which meant attention came more easily from men, and my husband seemed so proud to be by my side. I didn't realize it at first, but he was pushing me to flirt with other men and women as well. When it finally dawned on me, I asked him on the way out of the house one night if we were headed toward an open relationship. He replied that he thought we were.

My heart sank, but there was also relief. We were at a point where we didn't want to be together anymore, or at least that's where I was. Soon, we were spending quite a bit of time pursuing other people and outside interests, which, thankfully, took the pressure off worrying over each other or even having to see each other at all.

That entire segment of my life blurs through my memories like streaks of paint – wildly varied colors of supposedly fun things smeared across my mind by the people who helped me drink, laugh, and party my way through the isolation I felt in the midst of it all. Looking back all these years later with perspective, maturity, and a great deal less alcohol in my system, I can much more clearly see the red flags pointing to signs that I was living out a death wish.

Drinking was the order of the day, and there were plenty of mornings I woke up to beautifully bright, cheery sun rays beaming through my curtains and thought grimly, "Well. I made it to another day." Most mornings when I woke up with that thought, I honestly didn't know how I felt about it.

One part of me enjoyed the life I was living and craved the attention and fast pace. The other part of me relished the numbness of this life. The part that was once happy had become buried and now grimaced at new days thinking, "Great. Another chance to do it all again." There were plenty of days I woke up annoyed that I had to make the effort to breathe when I just wanted to return to sleep and not have to drag myself through it all once more.

A couple of months after we had that conversation on the way out, we were so disconnected from each other that he didn't even call me on my birthday to say "Happy birthday." We passed in the kitchen that morning as I left for work. He was coming in as I left even though I had no idea where he had been the night before, and, as usual, he offered no explanation.

Later that night, he had the audacity to act offended when he pulled up in the driveway and saw me leaving to go out with a friend. He acted as if I should have automatically assumed we would go out together to celebrate, even though I couldn't recall the last time we had done anything as just a husband and wife. The following morning, we spoke by phone and called it quits once and for all.

I was about to be divorced for the second time. After trying for years and going through fertility testing while he was in the military, we hadn't been able to have a child and had long since given up hope of conceiving. We considered adoption, but that, too, had fallen through. My soon-to-be ex-husband was leaving the state to be closer to his family and leaving me with bills I wasn't sure I could pay. My career was possibly coming to an end with the buyout of the hospital where I worked. Stressful uncertainty was just as much the order of the day as drinking. Having lost more than 120 pounds in the preceding year, I felt outwardly better and found myself once again filling life's gaps with attention from men, regardless of how I achieved it.

The married coworker who did shots with me at the bar one afternoon when a group of us sneaked out early and kissed me and put his hands all over me when we returned to the office for a meeting that night? I stopped him before it went much further, but I never told anyone and didn't feel too bad about it at the time.

The coworker who texted me some of the most hilariously depraved and inappropriately across-the-line things I've ever read about what he wanted us to do but was a model husband according to his wife? We were friendly outside work, and I have a mouthy, sarcastic sense of humor of my own. The attention was worth more than the feeling that the texts were unbefitting a professional relationship, especially during business hours, regardless of whether we were friends after work.

The friend with benefits who was also seeing one of my friends occasionally? She and I knew about each other and didn't mind. We laughed upon finding out he had asked us both to come to where he sold campers to pretend to look at one so he could use it as a front for having sex during work hours. We actually laughed. Things like that were funny. That was my life.

Meeting a former chat room friend in Dallas for a fun, flirty afternoon to reminisce and wish we were at different places in our lives while we were both still married? It seemed like no big deal. My husband was out of town and didn't care what I did with other people, and my friend's marriage had effectively been over for years as he had slept on his couch as long as I'd known him and had barely heard two words from his wife since right after their son was born. It never occurred to me no matter how much I cared about this person that it was still wrong.

Sharing guys, texting inappropriately with coworkers, stolen moments with married men that I didn't really feel bad about or at least tried not to. The decent, tenderhearted girl who grew up in small-town Southern Arkansas would not have been quite so nonchalant about those things. Deep down, I still wasn't, but it had become the life I knew. I covered my insecurities and failures and pain with bravado, fun, and tipsy escapades, and filled in the aching gaps in my life by reaching out one random moment at a time to connect with whoever would reach back.

Give me your spotlight! Give me your praise!
Worship me! Look at me!

Don't look at me…
Don't notice me…
I'm damaged and flawed and hurt…

Touch me! See me! Love me!
Don't you want to know me?!

God, what have I done…
Dear Lord, take me home…
Please don't let anyone want to know me tonight…

Most people who met me during that time did want to know me, though. I bordered on suffering from Multiple Personality Disorder – one person during the day who could juggle the responsibilities of a professional career and another person at night who could be whatever anyone needed her to be at any given moment and rise – or crawl through the depths of debauchery – to whatever the occasion required.

One night, I found myself perched on yet another barstool next to Chris, a guy I'd known for several months but who, up until about a week after this particular night, I didn't know was married. We were kissing inappropriately for being in a public place, as more than a couple of tequila shots can tend to inspire, especially when you've lost the will to care what the world thinks. Alan, the bartender, was Chris' friend and someone I'd met through the people my ex-husband and I were hanging out with a few months earlier. Alan had been giving us grief for about 30 minutes about our far-too-public display before he finally said, "Why don't you two get a room?" We stopped, looked at each other, laughed, and simply replied, "Okay!"

Alan followed us outside for a break as we left. Considering my surface-level relationship with both of them, I had an oddly false sense of security as we laughed and talked and enjoyed the cool fall night. Having known them both socially through friends for several months, there was a comfortable familiarity, even though I wouldn't have called either of them close friends. The longer we stood there, the more comfortable Chris became and the more his hands ran freely over me. It didn't take long to realize we needed to leave before things went any further. Alan made it clear he didn't want us to leave because that meant he had to go back to work.

"Take me with you," he said, jokingly, pouting and pretending he wanted to join us as we walked away hand in hand, giggling and still all over each other.

"Sorry," I said flippantly. "I don't hang out with boys. Only men!" I laughed at my own joke and thought he would surely respond by making a face or slinging a few cuss words my way, perhaps flipping me off as he sulked back to work.

In an instant, he stepped toward me, closed that four- or five-step gap before I knew what was happening, grabbed my arms, and yanked me away from Chris. It all happened so fast I couldn't fight my way out of it when he twisted my arms behind my back and began dragging me across the parking lot. Chris watched silently and did nothing to help.

I was far from silent.

All these years later, it's a blur what I actually said as it all happened so quickly in a cloud of dust and cussing, but I remember hollering for Chris to help me and to make Alan stop, demanding that he let me go, and feeling as if my arms were being pulled off. Several panicked minutes seemed to pass as he forced me across the parking lot, but it couldn't have taken more than a few seconds for him to drag me the 10 feet or so to where his motorcycle was parked near the bar door.

He bent me over the back of his motorcycle shoving my head down onto the seat and pinned me there with his elbow. With his free hand, he jerked the front of his pants down, slammed himself against me, and leaned over, pressing even harder and grinding as he said, "I'll show you the difference between a boy and a man."

His tone, the way he sounded slightly out of breath, the underlying demand in his voice – I was transported back to a dark, muggy room in Texas hearing Tyler tell me to say his name just one time so he could tell Phillip I knew it was him. I closed my eyes, held my breath, and felt years of tears, anger, and frustration boil to the surface.

In moments like that, everything slows down, even though you know realistically things are happening oh-so-quickly. All I could think as I lay there thrown over the back of his motorcycle was to wonder if this had somehow been a plan between Chris and Alan all along, and I had stumbled right into it. This was where I would be found the next day, and this was the last thing my parents would ever know about me. If this were going to be my last chance, I couldn't go down without a fight. I was in public and was determined to get someone's attention.

After letting the incident with Tyler play out in shock without fighting back, I wasn't going to let this become part of my brain's highlight reel in the same way. His words echoed through my mind saying he would show me "the difference between a boy and a man."

"Well, you're going to have to move because I can't see Chris from here," I managed to choke out, as he continued grinding against me, pushing my face into the bike seat, and almost lying on top of me by this point. Alan jumped up as soon as I said those words, shocked, angered.

He knew what I meant. He knew I was proclaiming that nothing he could show me and nothing he thought made him a man could compare to the man Chris was, even though Chris was acting more like a scared little boy who couldn't summon the courage to protect me or even attempt to speak up on my behalf from a safe distance. Chris had done nothing but stand on the sidelines watching the entire incident unfold.

Alan stepped back, arms up with an intensely confrontational "what in the hell did you say to me" attitude. Ignoring the fact that he is about five inches taller than I am and had just manhandled me across the parking lot as if it were nothing while I fought back, I charged at him with years' worth of frustration and rage erupting through my arms. Somehow, I overcame fear to summon the strength to push him several feet back against the building. I charged at him with one hand against his chest and the other against his throat. Without going into the distastefully explicit, four-letter-word-laden language I used, suffice it to say, I told him if he ever laid his hands or any other part of his disgusting body on me or so much as considered speaking to me again, it would be the last thing he ever did.

The way I reacted could have backfired if he hadn't been quite so taken off-guard. I didn't stop to think of what might happen if this man who could so easily have beaten me into the ground and left me for dead had snapped out of his frozen, open-mouth-staring astonishment. At that moment, I honestly didn't care how he reacted as long as he understood exactly how intensely, passionately, and unfalteringly I meant every one of the horribly heartfelt things I said.

For the first time, I fought back.

My words and actions said, "No. You will not treat me this way." It felt good. In fact, it felt extraordinary. Not since long before I was shocked out of a drunken haze into reality by finding someone I had only met in passing on top of me demanding I say his name had I felt anything approaching this much empowerment. My days in Texas, and in particular my sexual assault, had changed me as a person and altered my life in untold ways, but there were many other things and people who shaped me along the broken road between then and the night Alan dragged me across the parking lot kicking and screaming.

The naïve girl who grew up in church youth group activities every weekend couldn't live the life she was living and pray to God for forgiveness or ask for help out of the world she was wallowing in – how could He help someone like me? How could someone like me ever be complete and walk in His Light again? I believed in forgiveness and believed in faith and miracles – there just wasn't much left in me that felt worth saving. There were plenty of nights I set my alarm hoping I might not wake up when it went off and plenty of days I trudged along in three-inch heels and business clothes concealing my mental fog behind a relentless smile and a compartmentalized brain and heart.

Outwardly, most people couldn't tell – professional career, friendships, close family ties, all wrapped neatly askew in a seemingly good life. However, inside there was a frequent struggle to reconcile who I was with whom I had become and balance that with the person I needed to be in the world around me in order to maintain appearances. As it all swirled and I tried to function in the midst of so many changes in my life throughout all those years, the one constant was the on-again, off-again way I got the message that telling the stories of sexual assault survivors was my mission to complete. Still, I vowed it would never be my story to tell, and still, the song "Maybe God Is Trying to Tell You Something" seemed to follow me.

Except, sadly, all those years while I was suffocating under the weight of my secrets and shame, I rarely reached out to God. I rarely stepped back and took a minute to thank Him for simply allowing me to make it through or giving me a chance to press the off switch on that clock one more day and have one more chance to get it right. The fact that the song was still following me was, by my way of thinking, inconsequential because God Himself was going to have to come down for a face-to-face with me if I had any chance of listening.

What a waste of so many years.

Thankfully, that's not how our Higher Power works. When I finally stopped running, I realized He had been there with me all along, waiting patiently and never taking His eyes off me. All those times I woke up another day – much to my dismay – to turn off the alarm clock, were His way of saying, "I'm not done with you." All those times someone in my life grabbed me by the arm or pressed me against a fence or said something bad to me or treated me as Mr. Wrong or Tyler or Alan had, He was there to carry me through to the next moment and remind me that deep in my soul, I was still the same decent person I had been raised to be, even if I didn't believe it.

When I couldn't believe in me, *He still did.*

Whether you're a person of faith or not, when you face something like sexual assault that changes you so dramatically and so permanently, you ultimately have to find something inside you that resuscitates your center, your focus, your core, your *soul* – maybe you find it for the first time, or maybe you just need to find your way back to it. It's possible you'll have to continuously rediscover it and remind yourself how extraordinary it feels to marinate there and let a sense of restoration pass over you, even for a brief time. That's sort of the nature of grief and dealing with things that hurt so deeply and enduringly.

For me, when I pray, I'm reminded that people like Alan who felt the need to teach me a lesson over the back of his motorcycle are irrelevant in my life. When I hear Tyler's voice in my head, as I often do, I understand now that the words are simply echoes of a painful moment. They are not the soundtrack of my life. They have no bearing on the person I am or who I have the potential to be in life.

I sometimes walk away from my time of prayer feeling as if I have the strength to keep hearing those sounds or seeing those images in my head and accept them with dignity and grace and without worry. There are other moments, though, when I open my eyes and have the deepest sense of peace and strength. When that happens, I give myself permission to evict those images and sounds completely and walk away breathing air that is free from the past, even if in my weakness I tend to allow them back in eventually. When I feel that way, I know that no one has the right to be in my heart or mind unless I grant them space there, and I refuse to allow this man – or any other person – to dictate anything to me.

Through the process of writing this book, I accepted that I allowed the people and events that hurt me to come in and out of my life partially because of my own weaknesses and a desire to fill mental and emotional gaps and immaturities with all the wrong things and partially because of a disconnection from the path I knew God had for my life. That does not mean I withdraw responsibility from the people who did the dreadful things to me that took place through the years. On the contrary, I now indict them for their part in my misery and no longer pin all the blame on myself.

However, I accept that I allowed them to take their place in my life and didn't stop them when they hurt me or took advantage of what they saw as an easy mark. When you don't fight back against something, you validate it. You say, "I'm okay with this," even if your heart and soul are aching about the way you're being treated. Finding myself bent over the back of a motorcycle in a bar parking lot in the middle of the night and knowing I had to get up to go to my professional job the following morning and pretend none of it happened – and realizing this was what I had allowed my life to become – affected me in a very stunningly eye-opening way that night. I decided, in that single instance of standing up for myself, to own my power and strength for the first time and to never again let anyone put his hands on me unless I wanted them there. As simple as it sounds, I needed to give myself permission for that.

CHAPTER EIGHT

Choices

A week later, I was back at the same bar with a group of friends. My resolve to avoid alcohol and drama was strong, and I was enjoying hanging out talking to a male friend I hadn't caught up with in a while. We both noticed a guy in a gray sweatshirt and yellow baseball hat at the other end of the bar staring at us and smiling over his cigarette. My friend snickered.

"Do you want me to leave so Yellow Hat Cutie can come talk to you?" he asked.

The bartender slid a shot of tequila with a lime over to me. I laughed.

"I didn't order that," I told her and tried to slide it back. "Not tonight."

She slid it right back to me, rolled her eyes, and signaled to the end of the bar where Yellow Hat Cutie was grinning from ear to ear.

He nodded as if to say, "Enjoy."

"Oh, my gosh," I said, blushing with embarrassment. "He can't be more than 12. What should I do?"

"Talk to him," my friend said. "He looks sweet. Maybe his mom will hire you to babysit." He tried to hide his laughter as he walked away and left me standing alone at the bar.

Hesitant but thinking how good-looking the guy was and hoping maybe he would be different than other guys I'd met, I took the shot, smiled, and made my way over to sit on the stool next to him.

"Thanks, but I wasn't planning to drink tonight," I said. "At least let me buy you one." He pointed to his drink – a glass of soda.

When he explained he couldn't drink, I wasn't sure if he meant he was trying to quit, if he had a health problem, or if he couldn't afford to drink since he just spent his money on me. The look on my face must have given away my confusion because the bartender leaned across and explained with a grin that was clearly trying to hold back a laugh.

"He's not old enough to drink, honey. You caught you a young'un," she said.

Yellow Hat Cutie introduced himself with a handshake, and I had no idea I had just had first contact with one of my life's most influential people. At that moment, we were just two strangers hanging out on barstools chatting. He was sweet, just as my friend had joked, and there was clearly an age gap between us, 10 years in fact.

The difference was evident in our interests, in how we talked about things, and in many other ways.

But there was a kindness and a gentleness about him that drew me in. His eyes were thoughtful, and he listened attentively when I spoke. When he told me about himself, I wanted to know more. He was funny and had the most endearing laugh. He didn't flirt the way other guys did or say sexually inappropriate things, and he never tried to touch me or get overly close to me. I felt as if I were making a friend, but he was a friend who made my heart dance a little when he smiled as I talked.

Despite my insistence I wasn't going to drink, I had taken the shot. We continued talking, and when my friends and I decided to go to another bar, he joined us. We danced and laughed and mostly ignored everyone else. My life began to change because of a simple choice to accept a drink and see where the conversation went.

Because of that choice, life moved quickly in new directions. We were silly together and enjoyed getting to know each other. We went Christmas shopping and hung out with friends. We cooked dinner and watched movies. I stopped going out all the time and rediscovered a love of staying in. Being with him made me forget the recent demise of my five-year marriage and the fact that my professional life was up in the air. He was fun. He didn't expect me to be perfect. He didn't challenge me or argue with me. He was the opposite of everyone and everything in my life.

One day, I stopped by his apartment to surprise him with a birthday gift. He wasn't home and two hours later still wasn't there when

I stopped back by. It was his 21st birthday, so I assumed coworkers had taken him for a drink at the bar where we met. The bartender said she hadn't seen him. He didn't answer his phone, and no one knew where he was.

I found out the next day he had been in jail. While walking home the night before from the same bar, he had been stopped by an officer who asked what he was doing behind the building. During a routine search, the officer found a small amount of marijuana in his sweatshirt.

He was telling me all this after he was bailed out, of course. He had used his one phone call from jail to contact his best friend to ask him to call *me* – not to bail him out but to let me know where he was so I wouldn't be mad. Instead of trying to contact me, though, the friend arranged bail, just as he should have, so I was finding out what happened after it was all said and done.

I went to his apartment to tell him I had no desire to be with someone who was into that lifestyle. I had a stable job that required me to maintain a decent reputation, and even if I hadn't had that job, the one thing I *did* have at that stage in my life was enough respect to never put myself in a position to be dragged down to a negative place by someone who couldn't handle themselves.

But there he was with those pleading brown eyes gazing up at me while I told him all this, and out of those eyes trickled the most miserably unhappy little tears.

"I knew you were going to break up with me," he said.

Choices

Break up with you?
When did I officially become your girlfriend?

My brain told me to get off the couch, walk out the door, and never look back.

I couldn't.

As my brother once pointed out via Lisa Loeb lyrics, I have "compassion for strangers" and "affinity for danger," both of which were powerful enough forces to keep me rooted onto that couch listening to him plead his case of how it "would never happen again" and how he "would do anything" I wanted as long as I gave him another chance. I had to make a choice.

Brain. Heart. Brain. Heart. Brain. Which one to choose…

Go with what your brain tells you, Devan.
Get up. Walk to the door.
Make sure you give him a hurtful look
right before slamming the door
with every ounce of infuriated strength you have.
Be done with it. Move on.
You don't need this.

As crazy as it sounds now looking back, I'll always be thankful I didn't listen to my brain.

There were only a few more nights after that of hanging out with friends and drinking and a few more nights of not remembering who or where I was like there had been in the partying days, and even those nights weren't as scary. I finally had someone by my side watching over me and making sure I made it home, someone making sure I was cared for and safely tucked in my own bed out of harm's way at the end of the night.

Those party nights didn't feel necessary anymore. I had someone who had as many or more issues than I had. Taking care of him, playing house, and filling my days and nights with a more settled routine took the place of my death wish and gave me something outside myself on which to focus, even if giving up that crazy life ultimately meant trading my unresolved past problems for a whole new set.

We had so many rough moments in the year that followed. Two people who are so incredibly different and on opposite life paths attempting to force those paths to run parallel are surely going to forge a bumpy road now and then; however, there were also many laughs and good times, and because I stayed on that couch and let him keep talking, I found myself a year later embarking on the greatest, most rewarding journey of my life – motherhood.

If I'd chosen my brain and slammed the door as I imagined, the world wouldn't have my Katherine. After many years of trying to conceive a child with both my husbands and being told by physicians that conception was something I should give up, I abandoned my lifelong hope for a child. I doted on my friends, loved on my pets, and tried not to let it bother me. Every year on Mothers' Day, I hid under the covers until that hallowed, uterus-worshipping day passed to avoid having one more person ask me at a restaurant if I wanted the Mothers' Day discount or having anyone see me attempt to avoid all contact as I sat in the church pew quietly fighting tears when the mothers were asked to stand to be recognized.

I truly believed – and still do – that this man to whom I inexplicably gave a second chance was sent to my life by God Himself to save me from my wildin' days by giving me Katherine. No amount of turmoil and anguished tears and questioning why I let his brown eyes repeatedly manipulate me ever mattered again once I saw my baby's old-soul eyes open and look directly into mine for the first time. I knew right then and there my life would never, should never, and could never be the same again. Devan was Mama, and Mama's bruised and broken heart was finally whole and beating powerfully for the first time in years.

He didn't spend a great deal of time with us at the hospital when Katherine was born, but he was begrudgingly there, hangover and all, when we were discharged. Adjusting to life as a father was a shock, but he tried for a while. It wasn't that he didn't want to love her or be part of her life. Based on what he and a few of his relatives shared with me, I learned he had never had appropriate parenting role models, and he had never planned to be a father. In fact, the first thing he asked when I told him I was pregnant was, "What are you going to do about it?" Clearly, the experience was a shock from the first minute he found out, and his lack of interest in adjusting to it was evident in everything he did.

After trying to make our relationship work and separating a couple of times for brief periods, we ended our relationship when Katherine was six months old. To say it didn't end well is an understatement.

There were so many arguments and so much tension and frustrating life lessons I found along the ugly road of sharing life with someone who needed marijuana just to be able to function in his daily life, who grew up so differently than I had, and who had a history of other issues with which he struggled.

I learned unwanted lessons about court systems, filing police reports, working with lawyers, and how to understand protective orders. I cried many anguished tears and spent countless hours begging him to be the person he told me he *wanted* to be and *could* be that day in his apartment not long after we met. Ultimately, though, like most things in life, it all came down to choices.

I chose to stay with him when I knew it wasn't in my best interest. He chose negative consequences over the possibility of better options and a life with us as his family. I chose to remove him from our life and to raise Katherine by myself. He chose to threaten us and to keep floundering in addiction.

We both made choices.

I'm glad he chose me the night we met, and all these years later, I'm glad I listened to his plea that evening at his apartment. I'm glad I chose to spend time with him, to get to know him, to share a season of my life with him, and to create a beautiful miracle who calls me Mama.

Every day of life is another chance to make choices. These days, I prefer to step toward choices that end in more constructive, peacefully loving consequences. I'm working on the forgiveness part but make no promises on how long it will take me to fully get there. As people sometimes say, "Let go, and let God." It's in His time, not mine.

His time. Not *mine*.

I still struggle with this *Kairos* concept of things happening in God's time, but I'm trying. My brain says I could/should have control of my life by making good choices, but my heart is grateful I didn't listen to my brain when Yellow Hat Cutie had the bartender slide that shot of tequila over to me all those years ago.

*"Every day of life is another
chance to make choices."*

Chapter Nine

Waking Up

A couple of months after Yellow Hat Cutie and I ended our relationship, I began talking to Richard, *Mr. Right*, who is now my husband, the only man Katherine has ever known as a father, and the man whose adoption of her was finalized when she was 3. I had no plans to meet anyone or date again, but my path crossed with him one day when he sent me a casual message online.

We knew each other growing up in that small town in Southeast Arkansas, went to the same church, and graduated from the same school. Our parents still lived in the same town on opposite ends of the same street and went to dinner together just about weekly for years. To top it off, he and his brother were good friends with my brother in high school.

His message wasn't intended to be flirtatious or to see if I might be interested in going out. But he was, quite unintentionally that day, setting us on a path that led to marriage, two more remarkable daughters, and a life together that daily surpasses anything I could have imagined God would grant for me when I was in the depths of hopelessness and living out my death wish for so many years. Richard is the husband and father Katherine and I didn't know we could ever find.

I genuinely thought we were better off by ourselves trusting in our own strength and determination, but once again God had different ideas. Unlike my usual foolishness, for once, I listened to His guidance rather than my own stubbornness, and it made all the difference in our lives. It's in large part because of the empowering, reassuring love I've discovered since being married to Richard that I was able to step out on faith when my friend Ashley contacted me with her story of being assaulted and say, "Okay, God, I'm listening. I'm not running anymore. If you want me to write this book, guide me. Give me the words You want me to say, and let's help these survivors tell their stories."

Many men wouldn't have supported their wives' baring their souls in as transparent a way as I set out to. Discussing such graphic details of your personal life is not naturally comfortable, and many husbands would have been too embarrassed. It certainly hasn't been easy, and I know he struggled wanting to protect me from further pain and possible humiliation.

Unfortunately, grief and tears were an organic part of the development, and he waited patiently, never asking to read what I wrote, never demanding to have any sort of editorial input over the content and what I could and couldn't reveal. He isn't that guy. Richard is my greatest champion and my biggest fan, but the writing of this book put his patience and sympathy to the test in ways neither of us could have predicted. He understands, though: When God asks you to do something, you do it, even if you waited 18 years to get started.

One night when I first began writing and realizing hard truths about myself and the realities I had lived, we made love. Afterwards, I cried quietly in the bathroom trying to keep him from hearing my tears – not because I was sad or because I didn't enjoy being with him or because he said anything that upset me. In fact, it was exactly the opposite of all of those things. In an instant, in a sudden moment of revelation after years of blaming my brokenness and pain on waking up with a stranger on top of me, I recognized that I'd never truly appreciated the romantically sexual, intimate side of a relationship until I met Richard.

I finally understood that my wounds, some of which were self-inflicted, started long before Tyler entered my life or my body or my memories, long before his shaggy hair and slitty eyes were hanging over me in the dark, insisting I say his name. The mightily broken road that led me to his bedroom that night was paved with poor choices dating back to years earlier when I allowed myself to be controlled and abandoned by my first long-term boyfriend, followed by my first husband's verbal, emotional, and mental abuse. I realized also at that moment that they, along with the other men who had come into and out of my life through the years in one way or another, were each important parts of the fractured person I became, the person Richard had mended.

Luke was my first physical experience and was my fiancé for three years. Despite the obvious problems in our relationship, he was important. He patiently taught me about the sexual side of myself and the beauty there is to behold in the world when naïve eyes are opened. He inspired me with enough teenage audacity to stand up to my parents and make my own decisions, even if hiding our relationship wasn't the best way to go about it.

Richard is the most significant person ever to come into my life. He gave me faith in love, in people, in the security of strong arms around me. He helped me appreciate the astounding things God ordains for our bodies when we choose a single person with whom we want to share a lifetime of lovingly pure, honest dedication. He is my first *true* love, and he will remain *my only real love* – the person I'll spend the rest of my days cherishing and experiencing and feeling a connection with as I could never experience with anyone else.

Guys like Luke, Mr. Wrong, Tyler, Jeff, Tony, Yellow Hat Cutie, and others who came into my life in fleeting lessons served a purpose. They couldn't have been there if I didn't allow it, and some of them, like Jeff, seemed to have a revolving door in and out of my world. I was a trusting person with a gaping hole in my heart that I spent far too much time hoping to fill.

Like many young girls who buy into pop culture's idealized notion of Prince Charming and rose-scented romance, I thought people were basically good and that romance, love, and sex were essentially how they were depicted on the big screens of my childhood. I continually played back my life's moments days later like a highlight reel and wanted to live in a sitcom or teen movie like every other girl who grew up in the late '80s and early '90s.

Unfortunately, I also, on some level, believed my relationship role was not one of choice most of the time and that men had the upper, not-always-so-gentle hand. While my parents did their best to model a loving, balanced relationship, the world didn't always reinforce that message.

My parents taught me to be independent in career choices and to have my own mind, to study hard, and to go to college. They cautioned me that I needed to find a good job before settling into sharing life with someone so that if I were unexpectedly alone someday, I could support myself; however, without having spoken to my parents about sex and my role in a physical relationship, I filtered my lessons on sexuality and romantic empowerment through media, movies, television shows, gossip with friends, and my own perceptions of what I saw in the world.

Along the way, pop culture taught me things I'm certain my parents never intended for me to learn, and if the interviews I've conducted while preparing for this book are any indication, many women feel the same. Not only do we not want our daughters and sons who are growing up in today's world to receive these messages – we also don't want these messages filtering to the people they may someday encounter or with whom they may someday share their lives:

- Men are sexually dominant and should always take the lead. Women should never be the assertive one in the relationship. It's unladylike. Women don't "want" sex. That's for men.

- Men can't control themselves, so make sure you're always well covered – no exposed shoulders, low-cut shirts, skirts that rise more than two inches above your knees, etc. Showing skin tells the world you're "low-class" and "trashy."

- If you ever get the reputation for being a low-class/trashy girl (whether you "earn" it or not), you might as well give up ever being seen any other way. You're now one of "those girls," and every man will expect you to "put out" as soon as he meets you.

- It's the woman's responsibility to change her behavior so the man doesn't have to try to control himself. Don't give him a reason to want to act on his passions.

- In a sexual assault, the burden of proof will always be on the woman, and there are countless factors that can be brought up that will make it more difficult to prove her side of the case:

  ○ Was she in a location she shouldn't have been?

  ○ Was she drinking?

  ○ Did she lead him on?

  ○ Did her clothing choice make him think she wanted sex?

  ○ Did they discuss that they might engage in sexual activity even though she changed her mind before or after having alcohol and became unable to communicate effectively (or at all)?

  ○ Were they in a relationship and already interacting sexually or had she had sex with someone he knows?

These types of messages and many other similar messages young women still receive about sex are frightening as Richard and I contemplate sending our daughters into the world. In this supposedly enlightened age where people try to be more openly in touch with their feelings and strive for a more balanced life, middle schoolers are caught "sexting" nude pictures of themselves and charged with child pornography while parents defend it with "boys will be boys." The same people turn right around and "slut-shame" the girls who gave in to pressure from the boys and sent pictures. Middle schools keep boys and girls on opposite sides of their cafeterias and force them to enter and exit the schools through separate paths to avoid unnecessary interactions among what they perceive to be the out-of-control, hormonal rageballs they've been put in charge of wrangling seven hours a day.

Unfortunately, these types of behaviors, such as sexting, go on in the classroom just as much as they might go on in the cafeteria. They take place outside school hours, too, when adults don't monitor what children do or to whom they talk. In some cases, the adults are simply too technologically inexperienced to understand the need to know what's going on or how to monitor it. Perhaps even scarier is the fact that even though not all young people are involved in this type of behavior, we allow the media and pop culture to normalize the idea that they are, which causes many to believe it's what they should do, too.

If it's what everyone is doing, what harm could there be?
It's just one picture.
He said he loves me, and I know
he won't show it to anyone.

Everyone is having sex, even kids my age.
I see it on television all the time.
Every song on the radio is about sex.
It'll be fine.

When the pervasive messages and images our young people receive are sexual in nature, their understanding of what's acceptable becomes skewed. These messages become normalized – sex is power, promiscuity is exciting, sexting is a private way to show someone you care. While we are quick to blame social media and the Internet for the normalization of these concepts, that is not necessarily true. While it might make it a faster process, the advent of social media, cell phones, and young people who can get around their world both literally and digitally much faster than they once could isn't to blame for the normalizing of these attitudes and behaviors.

Growing up in the '80s and graduating from high school in the early '90s before technology was as prevalent as it is today, I was just as overwhelmed by negative stereotypes and sexual normalizing that affected my opinions about who I was and how I was supposed to act in a relationship as I carried myself out into the world. My parents taught me right from wrong, as most loving parents do – for example, I knew I shouldn't let someone hit me. When a boy raised his hand to me in high school, I didn't flinch.

He was in an argument with a man who said something rude to him and flirted with me at a gas station on Homecoming night. I begged him to ignore it and get back in the truck, but instead, they got into a heated argument and began threatening each other. When he didn't listen to my continued pleas to leave, I jumped out of the truck, high heels in hand, and walked quickly across the parking lot toward home. He walked after me yelling for me to come back as I took off running.

Unfortunately, I couldn't run quickly in bare feet across a rough parking lot, so it didn't take him long to catch me. When he caught up, grabbed my arm, and spun me around with his hand in the air to hit me while a small crowd looked on with mouths gaping, I couldn't have cared less. The straight-A, goodie-two-shoed, never-breaks-a-rule, scared-of-her-own-shadow-and-Daddy's-too girl planted her feet ready to fight back. That still-confident young girl who had not yet been broken down by her own choices all but dared him to hit her, and defiantly wished he would.

I told him something along the lines of, "Hit me. When my Daddy gets done with you, there won't be anything left for that guy to go after." I couldn't wait to see what kind of greasy puddle would be left after I took my shots and then told Daddy what he had done.

My Daddy didn't raise a fool or – when push came to shove – a fearful daughter.

What my Daddy had accidentally raised without realizing it, though, was a sheltered young lady who let the world tell her things about which she should have known better. While I would never have allowed someone to hit me, it was not outside the realm of possibility I would allow a man to push me around sexually simply due to lack of experience, knowledge, and my misguided understanding of my role in a physical relationship. I was inexperienced and extraordinarily uneducated. My perceptions about what was realistic and expected were misshapen by what I had seen in the world around me and what pop culture had normalized.

Hollywood showed me drunk women being taken advantage of and later forgiving the guy or falling for him in two of my favorite teen movies. I watched teenage boys on the big screen set up video cameras in several movies to watch teenage girls undress, and those scenes are still, to this day, popularly believed to be hilarious on an iconic level.

In a movie commonly thought to be one of the most romantic of all time, the hero is persistently told "no" by the leading lady, but he won't accept her response. He pretty well makes a jerk of himself trying to convince her to change her answer, and the viewer is led to believe his behavior is acceptable and that we should cheer his actions because we believe the horizon holds a happy ending if she will just give in. Hollywood also introduced us to lyrics like "Did she put up a fight," which is still sung today in high school productions of *Grease* all over the country. No one bats an eyelash or stops to think of what we're reinforcing to young people through this "classic."

I don't believe we should burn all those movies or erase history. That's unnecessary. Do these things happen? Of course, they do. Do we have to continue allowing them to be the pervasive attitudes in our culture? Certainly not.

When viewed, they offer an opportunity for openly transparent conversations with young people about what they've seen and heard. If we aren't having these conversations, we're further reinforcing the messages every time they're played and increasing the likelihood that the attitudes of the past will perpetuate into the future. I pray this will stop. If you're a sexual assault survivor, you've probably prayed similar thoughts.

Dear God,
Let people understand.
Don't let them go through what I went through.
Let their eyes be open to why they must talk
openly and honestly about sex and what's right and wrong.
Make them see that they have to stop allowing their bodies
to be treated like worthlessly expendable pieces of garbage.
When we value ourselves and expect better treatment,
we will value each other more as well.
Please, God, let them see that this isn't acceptable.
We need change without suffering to understand why.

People don't always comprehend why things are hurtful if they haven't experienced similar things themselves. I've brought up the topic of sexual assault and the need to educate youth about the dangers of normalizing negative sexual stereotypes in a politely questioning, non-confrontational way and been stared at as if I were swinging a burning bra and had some sort of foreign feminist language tattooed on my forehead inked with the blood of all men who dared to cross my path. And surely while doing that I was also proclaiming that all movies and newborn males must henceforth be burned in the town square. I'm not sure if the people who looked at me that way were uncomfortable with the topic, worried I might share a personal story, or simply thought the whole idea was too much to talk to young people about. It was probably a combination of all of the above. Most people don't want to talk about sex or anything to do with physical relationships, but it's a topic that deserves to be discussed.

Just as our society has normalized negative sexual stereotypes, the tide must turn toward normalizing open discussions about sex, safety in how relationships are approached, how to protect against diseases and unwanted pregnancies, abstaining until the appropriate time, learning it is okay to say "No" to anyone at any time even if you have engaged in sexual contact with that person before, the difference between consent and coerced consent, and so many other relevant topics.

Until we begin talking to our young people, and many adults who are still in the dark about this topic as well, there will continue to be countless people like me who dwell in the land of, "Well. I made it to another day." They'll wish they hadn't. They'll continue to fight the mental and emotional demons from where they have been and what they have done in the name of filling gaps in their lives or trying to make other people happy.

I'm a sexual assault survivor, not a brainless idiot. I wasn't stupid. *I promise I wasn't.* Clearly, I knew I shouldn't allow myself to be raped. If a stranger had attacked me in a dark alley as we see on crime shows or in the movies, I would have fought back at all costs, and I would have immediately gone to the hospital and reported the crime to the police.

But that isn't what happened.

My brain told me the reality was that I was just another drunk girl who should've known better. I stupidly slept with two guys in one night and eventually returned to reality enough to call the second one by the right name. I didn't scream or fight back. I grabbed my clothes and left hurriedly in what pop culture calls the morning-after "walk of shame." I showered until my skin was about to peel off, but I didn't cry, most likely because I was numb and in shock, but who can prove that anyway? Because of all those things – all those ways that I didn't react as the world told me I should have if I had *really* been assaulted – I knew nobody would have believed me if I reported it. On the outside, anyone would have thought I didn't even care.

But I cared. *A lot.*

I still do, and I always will.

"Like many young girls who buy into pop culture's idealized notion of Prince Charming and rose-scented romance, I thought people were basically good and that romance, love, and sex were essentially how they were depicted on the big screens of my childhood."

Chapter Ten

We are More

The people introduced in the following chapters cared, too, even though most of them never reported, or even spoke about, their assaults. Like me, many of them didn't immediately see themselves as victims or assumed no one would believe them, so they grieved in silence. They privately healed. They swept their mental and emotional debris under the rug as well as they could. They went on with their lives – some of them compartmentalizing their assault for years without permitting themselves to think about it, and some of them rarely letting a day or perhaps an hour pass without replaying it in their minds.

Regardless of which reality they call their own, they're all in one key category: SURVIVOR. It has been an honor to record their stories and to share my own with each of them. Throughout this journey, I found a stronger, less broken road that led to my own healing, and I believe giving these survivors much-needed voices helped them heal on a deeper level as well.

God tried to tell me something for so long, and I finally stopped running and listened. Now, as we turn the pages of this book together and see the stories we are bravely sharing with the world – many of us telling them for the first time in detail – we can all heal in our own ways with the Father's arms stretched around us. If you have a story tucked away in the confines of your past and find yourself reflected somehow in these chapters, you may be prompted to explore your story in some small but significant way or perhaps to tear down walls and confront the past head-on.

Whatever you do, I pray you find solace and peace sooner than later.

If you share your story with someone, choose someone trustworthy who will listen with genuine care and concern for the person you have become since your assault. Make sure you speak to that person in the right time and place. If your chosen person is someone who may struggle with hearing what you have to say, consider choosing a neutral location like a park or counseling center rather than a personal space, such as a home or office.

However you proceed if you need to share a story of your own, proceed with caution. In today's culture, many people accept sexual assault survivors with compassion and consideration, but there are still many skeptics, perhaps due in part to the volume of people now openly talking about assault and using social campaigns such as #metoo to share their stories. Rather than allow survivors to come forward and to try to understand why they waited to tell their stories – for the first time they feel they live in a world where they *can* – the cynics question their motives.

- "You mean to tell me she waited all these years to tell someone she was raped? Give me a break! Anyone with half a brain would've run straight to the police as soon as it happened."

- "If it were me, I would've come up fighting. I sure wouldn't have just laid there."

- "We all know nothing happened to her. She just regrets having sex with him."

- "A guy said he was assaulted? That's the biggest lie ever. Guys can't be assaulted. What kind of man lets himself be assaulted?"

- "Date rape?! How could he rape her? I thought they were in a relationship."

- "She's always been the town slut – now she's an attention whore, too. This assault stuff is the latest bandwagon, and she loves a good bandwagon. You know how she is."

The list goes on. *And on.* It gets unpleasant. Names get called. Feelings are damaged, sometimes irreparably. The "town slut" turned "attention whore" example? While partially paraphrased, it is, unfortunately, not made up to exaggerate the point. It is, in fact, a real-life example of a judgmental person second-guessing someone who shared their #metoo moment via social media.

Partially because of years of damaging self-talk and partially because of the echoes of cynical statements such as these, it took me a long time to be ready to disclose to my family and friends. Accepting that they would never fully understand why I didn't talk to them when it occurred was something that didn't come easily. Even now,

I struggle with the feeling that I betrayed their friendship, loyalty, confidence, trust – all of which are centrally key components of strong relationships.

Finding the courage to reveal years of painful secrets was not a moment that arrived in my life accompanied by the feeling of deliverance for which I had prayed. A different sort of emotional barrier materialized as the words I was saying piled up around us. Even now, after telling my story at conferences, writing this book, and telling my family, there are still times when the walls my secrets built seem to be more tangible than ever. Whereas in the past those secrets were only walling me in, they are now out in the open where everyone can see them, walk around them, inspect them, and judge them, and we're all confined not-so-cozily into one small space as I stand in the middle with a spotlight glaring above me.

Nobody makes me feel that way other than me. Survivors have repeatedly shared that they are their own worst enemies and critics when it comes to permanently putting away the pieces of their assault and moving on to a restored, whole life with a fresh perspective.

"No one sees his face when it's in my mind, but it's enough to stop me in my tracks. Sometimes I feel like everyone sees the weird little slow-motion video of that night when it plays on loop in my brain," Elisa told me. Her story is Chapter 13. She hesitated to tell her story because of the pain of revealing her truths after so many years to family and friends. "Nobody can understand what it was like or why I didn't fight or why I didn't report it. It really doesn't feel like it's worth trying to explain, you know what I mean? But I have to. I need someone who loves me to understand."

I know that feeling. Undoubtedly, many survivors do. While we want someone who loves us to understand what happened, we also want to still be seen as *more* than what happened.

WE ARE MORE.

During interviews for this book, Jessica, the survivor featured in Chapter 16, perfectly summed up how it feels to talk to friends and family after an assault.

"For a while, I felt like people who knew what happened couldn't look at me without seeing The Girl Who Was Assaulted. It was my 'thing,'" she said. "You want them to just see you, but that isn't always possible. They find out this really hard truth, and they suddenly have their own issues to deal with, like, 'Could I have done something?' or maybe 'Why didn't she confide in me sooner?' It creates this totally bizarre energy between you."

As loved ones work through those feelings, they often wonder what they can do to help survivors move past the assault. That push to help can become the focus of their interactions for a brief, or perhaps even extended, period of time. Ashley, who helped inspire this book and is introduced in Chapter 11, said she continuously deals with well-intentioned people who advise her to stop socializing with her attacker.

"I see him a couple of times a month, and my friends think I'm crazy for not freaking out every time he comes near me," Ashley said. "It's a reality I accepted a long time ago. I made up my mind I wasn't going to let what happened affect where I went or who I shared my time with. If that means he's around sometimes, then whatever. My friends think that by hiding from places he might be, I'll be moving on from what he did, but that isn't going to help. Maybe that's what they would do, but that doesn't work for me."

Once an assault has been revealed, it can feel like a barrier around personal relationships. When a survivor interacts with a friend or family member after a disclosure, the barrier gate has to be opened to allow the person into the inner sanctum to talk and to feel bonded. Without allowing the person into that personal space, communication must take place through the now seemingly tangible barrier that previously existed only in the survivor's mind. The walls are now more than just imagined. They have become real, rigidly palpable, and potentially destructive to relationships if left unaddressed.

Talking to my family was far more challenging than talking to friends, especially when it came to telling them that so much of my life would be discussed in detail. For me, healing involved confronting things that dated back to my teen years and first marriage, and it included discussing previous relationships, poor choices, and other sexual encounters.

But good Southern folks don't talk
about that sort of thing!
We keep our crazy hidden where it belongs,
don't you know?

Sadly, I do know. It's that "some things don't need to be talked about" mentality that kept me silent through an overbearing first real boyfriend/fiancé, an emotionally/verbally/mentally/fiscally abusive, cheating first husband, waking up with a stranger on top of me, a string of less-than-kind men who rotated in and out of my life, getting dragged kicking and screaming across a bar parking lot and bent over the back of a motorcycle, a husband who wanted an open relationship, and the brief relationship with my oldest child's biological father against whom I now have a permanent, 500-yard restraining order.

After many mentally struggling years and a whole lot of prayer, I finally realized I am more than all those things, and I won't be silent about them anymore. I can't be. For my daughters. For their children. For the women and men who still live in silence. For the survivors whose stories have now had life breathed into them for the first time in these pages.

We are more than what happened to us, and we will not be silent. We will no longer allow those moments to play on repeat in our minds as our attackers go on with their lives without consequence. Even if the only justice we will ever have is in knowing our stories are spoken anonymously in these pages and that our attackers are brought to justice in our own minds and made to pay for their crimes in our hearts, then so be it. Through the voices we have shared, we are strong, we are proud, and we will never be silent again.

WE. ARE. MORE.

"After many mentally struggling years and a whole lot of prayer, I finally realized I am more than all those things, and I won't be silent about them anymore."

CHAPTER ELEVEN

Ashley

Ashley is my Divine inspiration. Without her call telling me what happened between her and her former fiancé, Stephen, I would never have stopped running from what I knew all those years that I was supposed to do. Because of the importance of her role in the writing process, I naturally wanted her to be the first interview.

The day we finally found time to talk, Ashley sat nervously in the oversized black leather chair across from me with her feet tucked under her, fidgeting with her phone despite knowing I already knew many of the details of her story. Her voice cracked a few times as she spoke.

"It was last summer," she began. "I had just received a really good bonus check, so a few of the girls from work and I went out and had double-shot margaritas. I've known one of the girls a really long time, so she and I went to another place after that where we had two or three vodka shots."

She paused and looked away momentarily, as if telling her story had begun to wear on her already, as if she had just heard out loud for the first time how much alcohol she had consumed that night.

"We went to a bar because there was a band playing, and by the time we got there, you'd think with all the alcohol we'd had, we'd be drunk," she said, "but we weren't feeling anything. We had more shots and drinks. Later that night, I knew there was no way I was going to drive home."

Ashley's story is familiar to many women out for a fun night with friends – alcohol, drink after drink spread out over an evening with seemingly little or no effect until suddenly, they find themselves needing help. Ashley said she didn't worry about it because there were quite a few people she knew at the bar, and Stephen, someone she trusted, was among them.

That night was one of only a handful of times Ashley and Stephen had been in the same social space since calling off their engagement because she tried to avoid him and his friends. According to Ashley, when the relationship ended, Stephen's friends blamed it on her and seemed to be everywhere she went – restaurants, theaters, grocery stores, bars, even her workplace – "reminding me how repulsive they thought I was."

Even worse, their verbal attacks weren't saved for when Ashley was alone. They had no problem sharing how they felt in front of her friends, family, and even her young daughter. They made Ashley's life increasingly difficult over the years, and she finally withdrew with her daughter into a lower profile life to avoid confrontation.

"There were so many of his friends there that night, and I always thought they all hated me," she said, "but at that point, they were all wanting to be my friends and wanting to hang out. I was thinking, 'Oh, finally! Ten years of most of this town hating me. This is all finally going to be over.'"

The friendly atmosphere, the unexpectedly kind exchanges of words, the lack of ridicule – Ashley's guard was down, and she knew she couldn't drive herself home. She was relieved when Stephen approached her and said, "You can come to my house. I've got a spare room. You can stay with me. It'll be fine. I'll take care of you."

By the time they left the bar, the ride to his apartment was a blur.

"I remember closing my tab out. I sort of remember being put in the back of a cab, and I don't remember anything else until I woke up with him on top of me," she said, pausing and taking a sighing, deep breath to let the image clear from her mind.

"I started crying, and he yelled at me and was like, 'Why are you crying' and got really upset. I don't remember anything after that until getting up the next morning and putting on my clothes and trying to leave."

Ashley said Stephen confronted her and became infuriated, loudly demanding, "Why are you leaving?" and "I don't understand why you're leaving!"

Remembering her car was still at the bar, Ashley retreated to the living room to call friends who could pick her up. When a close male friend finally arrived, she walked from the apartment to the front gate "…with no shoes looking just terrible and crying. It was the worst, and it was all I could do to keep my friend from going inside there once he realized why. He was trying to make fun of me when he first saw me and was saying, 'Look at you with your walk of shame.' Then he saw how upset I was and tried to get out of the truck to go in there to confront him."

Ashley said she does not recall consenting to having sex with Stephen and that it isn't something she would have agreed to under normal circumstances. All she remembers is waking up to find him inside her and that he became unexpectedly irate when she cried.

Unfortunately, she passed back out and doesn't recall what took place after that. It wasn't until the following morning when she got home and bruises started emerging that she realized how rough the interaction between them had been. She was especially concerned about the large, dark bruises on her breasts.

"I was just covered in bruises everywhere," she said, "and that doesn't come from normal sexual activity. I took a picture of them and sent it to him. I texted, 'So do you want to tell me what happened?' and he said, 'I don't know what that's from' and just blew it off."

She paused once more to regain her composure, a common trait I noticed among the sexual assault survivors who told me their stories and something I found myself frequently needing to do as I wrote my own story. The extended pauses, deep breaths, and long sighs usually preceded rationalization, reconciliation, or some form of personal forgiveness or moment of clarity.

This time was no exception.

"Honestly, I don't think he meant to do me any harm," she said sadly, quietly. "I don't think that was his intention, but it's just the fact that he was so cavalier about it. We both had so much to drink. Of all the people that I know, I would've never thought *him*."

She showed me a picture of her bruised breasts. *I shuddered.*

Even though I had known of the picture's existence for more than a year before I saw it firsthand and had heard it described, seeing the extent of the bruising took my breath away. Ashley explained that she bruises somewhat easily but that these particular bruises were deep, dark, and painful and had lasted three and a half weeks.

Not long after the assault, as she was sifting through the emotional and mental aftershock, Ashley confided in two friends, Robert and Audrey, a married couple who were close mutual friends with her and Stephen. They were among the few people she had been able to remain friends with after the breakup, and they had grown quite close despite the breakup's awkwardness.

"They could tell something was up," Ashley said, "and so I told them about it. I was talking to Robert at the bar one night, and Stephen was there. He showed Robert the picture I'd sent him of my bruises and made fun of it. He didn't know Robert knew about it all. Robert shut him down and walked away. He came over to me and said, 'I don't understand. I don't know this person. I don't understand who this even is anymore. Why would he show me this and act like it's not a big deal?' It's really sad when another man who's one of your best friends obviously realizes what you did is wrong, and *you* can't understand what you did is wrong."

Robert and Audrey stayed away from Stephen for the rest of the night. Robert told Ashley he couldn't help but wonder how Stephen's opinion of him could be so low that he thought the picture was something he would find interesting. He and Ashley questioned how this man they had known and respected for years could be barely a shadow of the person they once knew. Ashley left the bar in tears, remembering her assault and feeling the sting of humiliation knowing her assaulter had kept the picture of her bruised breasts and thought it held comedic value worthy of sharing openly in public.

Ashley never confided in anyone beyond her closest friends about the assault, and she and Stephen continue to see each other now and then in social situations. Because his friends began treating her more respectfully and stopped openly ridiculing her, she decided to resurface into the social light even though it means running into Stephen. I asked what that feels like and how she deals with it.

"I try to…I just think of it like a completely different person… that I don't relate…that he's somebody that…that it's not the same person I'm looking at that did that," she stumbled through the words, searching for a way to explain how she tolerates being sociable with the man who took advantage of her, openly made fun of her, and showed pictures of the aftermath so callously.

I asked if Stephen has ever talked to her about that night or if he tried to apologize or admit he might have thought she was more aware of what was happening. To my astonishment, she said he tried to rekindle a relationship with her not long before our interview.

"So, no understanding of what took place between you as something that was hurtful?" I asked.

"No remorse," Ashley replied flatly.

"No acknowledgement of anything? Just complete, 'Didn't happen.'"

"Yep," she responded and turned her phone around once more to show me the picture of her bruised breasts that appear as if she were forcefully held down to keep her immobilized for an extended period of time. "And he still texts me from time to time wanting to know if I want to get together."

She put her phone down and looked away.

"Do you think there will ever come a point when you'll cut him out of your life?"

This time, she didn't hesitate. It seemed to be an answer she had pondered at length, and I did not receive the answer for which I had hoped.

"I think if I did, it would cause more problems than just keeping him at arms' length because it's just now to the point where all these people I see on a very regular basis speak to me like a normal person. Before, they were constantly throwing insults at me in public. That's why I didn't do anything for years. I stayed away. I don't want to live like that because of other people. I want that to be my decision if I decide I don't want to do anything."

I asked if she could ever truly forgive him for what happened. She looked around once again, fidgeted some more with her phone but never answered.

"Would you believe him if he actually did apologize?"

"After this length of time, I don't know if I would believe him because he's made no mention of it. He acted like it didn't matter back then," she said. After a long pause, she added hesitatingly, "I don't think I would believe him."

Seeing that she was ready to move on from these questions, I turned attention from her assault and the immediate aftermath to the long-term effects, such as how she approaches teaching her daughter about sexual assault. When I asked if her assault affected how she explains relationships and men to her daughter and what she wants her to know as she grows up, Ashley said the incident with Stephen will not change how she approaches parenting her daughter through the teen years and learning about sexuality.

"Even before this, I knew there was a possibility of things like that happening because honestly most men don't care," Ashley said. "They really don't. Especially being as single as I am, it's just the kind of men I encounter. They're terrible. At work, one of our delivery drivers was a different driver one day, but it was someone we've had deliver for us when I worked at a different place. He said, 'Girl, you're still beautiful,' and I just replied, 'Uh huh, okay, thanks.' He left and came back because he forgot a box, and I was trying to be friendly and kind of being funny and said, 'Oh, you just wanted to see me again.' He said, 'If I only wanted to see you, I'd get your number. I'd take you out to dinner.' I laughed and ignored him because I knew he was married, but he had the nerve to turn around and add, 'No, I wouldn't take you out to dinner. I'd let you be my dinner.'"

She made a disgusted face at the thought of what the delivery driver said to her and told me comments like that are not uncommon from men who come into her workplace.

"No! We don't know each other like that for you to say things like that, *and* this particular guy is married. Most of the guys who come in there are. They're looking for something for their wife or girlfriend. I'm sure those trusting women wouldn't like knowing the men in their lives are talking to other women like that, but that's the way men are. That's the way they speak to you," she said.

Despite the calming deep breaths needed to get through the details of her story, the woman sitting across from me was self-assured and not at all embarrassed. I could tell she had drawn strength from her time since the assault and was in a better place than when she first contacted me. She had taken time to process, to filter her thoughts and emotions, to figure out the new boundaries of her interactions with Stephen.

She doesn't openly radiate as much as she once did, though. The woman I knew before the assault all but sparkled with light and love no matter when you saw her. On the day of our interview, the woman across from me still had a charm in her eyes, but she was different. Still glowing with a beautifully stunning light but tempered with a newfound discernment and sensitivity about the world, she now operates with more restraint and caution.

"Did the assault change your relationship with other men? Do you think it changed your trust factor? Does it change how you act when you go out?"

Her answer was clear and unhesitating.

"Oh, definitely," Ashley said. "I didn't drink for a long time at all because when you're in that situation and feel like you were so impeded by drinking, you feel totally helpless. I would never again drink so much that I couldn't drive myself. I'll have maybe one drink."

Ashley said she is constantly aware of who is around her when she goes out because she never knows who can be trusted.

"I keep an eye on people a lot more now," she said. "A *lot* more."

I got the impression she keeps her eye on people and her heart to herself. She would never say that, perhaps because she doesn't consciously realize it's a choice she's making or perhaps because she doesn't want to admit the assault cultivated a certain level of detachment in her personality where potential love interests are concerned. Unlike survivors who shut themselves off from relationships, though, Ashley says she is open to finding love and to the possibility of meeting someone with whom she can share her life, her laughter, and her once ever-present energy that now seems more reserved for those who earn it.

And it will take someone unquestionably extraordinary and beyond reproach to earn that love, if she chooses to share it. I believe she will someday when the time is right, and I pray Stephen someday realizes what he lost by taking advantage of his former fiancée when she was too intoxicated to consent. If he ever finds love of his own or has a daughter whose life he is privileged to guide, I pray he looks back on that night with Ashley and on his actions and realizes why she was hurting, not just physically, but mentally and emotionally.

Consent is key. I pray Stephen someday understands that, and I pray Ashley gives herself consent to forgive and to allow someone else to help her light radiate once again.

"I remember closing my tab out. I sort of remember
being put in the back of a cab, and I don't
remember anything else until I woke
up with him on top of me."

Chapter Twelve

Casey

"My grandfather would always say, 'Casey, your best friends are your paycheck and your mama, and you got the raw end of the deal on the mama part, so your best dependence is on that paycheck. You can't put your stock and your happiness in *him*. He isn't going to make you happy.'"

The slender, smiling woman sitting across from me had spent nearly two hours telling me some of the most tragic stories of abuse, sexual assault, and physical and psychological trauma I'd heard since starting this book, and she had a smile on her face.

A smile.

She laughed to herself often when talking about her grandfather. Any time she mentioned "PawPaw," a sincere smile softened her face and relaxed her sometimes anxious breathing for a few seconds.

Casey described PawPaw as her "angel." The "him" he told her not to put stock in fathered a daughter she became unexpectedly pregnant with in her mid-20's after years of turmoil that had led her to believe she couldn't have children. Much like my story, it's important to know what led Casey to that man's door.

Unlike my story, though, Casey's story began when she was an innocently trusting child.

"My mom and dad divorced when I was 2," she said. "They tried to make it work. He hung around a little while, and when I was around age 3, he finally left. That was it. I never had any contact with him again. By then, Phyllis, my mom, had already married Bruce."

That was when years of sexual, physical, emotional, mental, and verbal abuse began.

"My earliest very vivid memory that I have of sexual abuse with my stepdad was when he was in the bathtub, and he made me get in the bathtub with him," Casey said. "A few minutes into being in the tub with him, my mother came home. The way our bathtub was, it was an old-school trailer we were living in, and it had sliding mirror doors. He slid the door shut just enough so she couldn't see that I was in there, and he told her, 'I'll be out of the tub in a few minutes.' He forced me to give him oral sex, and he got out of the bathtub."

Casey said Bruce's rule for her was that she had to stay in the bathtub with the sliding doors closed until the water was cold before she could get out.

"He said that would give enough time for everybody to not real-ize what was going on," she said. "Later on in life, I found out he also abused both his sons in a previous marriage."

Her contempt is clear for this man who was supposed to fill a paternal, protective role in her life. According to Casey, the abuse continued for years. Phyllis was an alcoholic, and there were many nights she didn't come home from work. She went to bars or, as Casey said, "Wherever she would end up, and that was when Bruce would take his opportunities. It would vary from over-the-clothes things to not-over-the-clothes things. That started from a very early age. It was almost a regular, everyday basis."

Casey said, "I can tell you story upon story, night over night. There were times when we would get a phone call that some random person has found my mother in the back of a bar parking lot, and we needed to go get her, so Bruce would load us up in the truck to go pick her up. The whole way there I'm being forced to perform sexual acts on him. There was one night in particular that we went to go get her from a house where she was having an affair, and he brought us with him to show us that women are nothing but trash and that's why we get treated the way we do."

While Bruce was regularly assaulting and abusing her, his son Josh "took his turn with me," Casey said. "That was when I was about 9 or 10 years old. He was around his teen years. He was probably experimenting in a bad way from the lessons he learned from his father."

Casey said Josh was never an everyday member of the family, but, "When he swooped in, he swooped in like a tornado and left like a tornado, and my world would be rocked for several weeks. I think that he – and maybe this is my brain trying to come up with a reason why he did it – was trying to watch movies and reenact those things because the way he acted was never the way Bruce acted. It was never forceful. It was more like, 'I'm trying to do what everybody else does and what I see on TV, like let's make love.'"

Abuse was Casey's normal. It was her main view of what a family looked like since before she was school-aged. Her father had abandoned them without looking back, her mother was in and out and not truly present even when she was there, and her grandparents lived next door but were oblivious to what was going on. In the midst of it all, Casey was forced to be a parent to her sister, who is three years younger.

Her sister was often the target of Bruce's attention, but when Casey caught him going in her sister's room, she tried to redirect his attention and affection instead to shield her.

"I spent a lot of time protecting her and probably endured a lot more molestation and abuse because of it," Casey said. "There were times I would get beat because I wouldn't allow him to be alone with her. My mother was just never around. With that being said, she did know what was going on."

Casey said when she was around 9 years old, Phyllis walked into her room one night while Bruce was on top of her "...fully penetrating me. That was the downhill slope of (Phyllis and Bruce's) relationship, but it didn't stop anything. They started falling apart."

Not only did it not stop the abuse, but Phyllis also permanently left the home and moved several hours away leaving her daughters with Bruce because, as she explained when she left, she didn't want them to change schools. Casey said it was difficult for family members to intervene and demand that the girls be removed from Bruce's custody after Phyllis left because, from the outside looking in, everything was fine.

"We never really wanted for anything," she said. "He took care of his other three kids, so when everything started to fall apart, and with my mother being the alcoholic that she has always been, no one has ever believed anything she's ever said in her life."

About a year later, Phyllis and Bruce were divorced. Casey finally gathered the courage to tell her grandparents some of what was going on with Bruce. As many people of their generation might have been, they were not prepared for the conversation.

She started by talking to her grandmother.

"My grandfather was a very closed-off person, as many men are, especially of that age. He believed certain things are not to be talked about. I was always very afraid to talk to him about it, although he was also my savior in so many aspects of my life. I went to my grandmother and mentioned something to her about being abused, and she told me I needed to talk to my grandfather. PawPaw was beside himself. We grew up next door to my grandparents, and Bruce was still living there at this time directly next to their home. My grandfather went crazy, as you can expect, and went over there."

Casey said she still does not know what was said or what happened that afternoon. Her grandfather simply told her that he "said his piece" and that Bruce was supposed to leave her alone and stay away from all the grandkids.

The following week, her grandfather rearranged his work schedule to be at the house when Casey and her sister arrived home from school. Two days that week, though, he did not make it home before the bus dropped them off. The first day, Bruce was there waiting on the girls in the yard – something he had never done before that day.

"I just remember the feeling of dread not knowing what to expect but just knowing something bad was about to happen," Casey said. "I told my sister, 'Just go to MawMaw and PawPaw's.' She said, 'But there's nobody there.' I said, 'PawPaw should be home. You just go on up there. I'm going on in here and get some stuff, and I'll be over there in a few minutes.' As I came up the hill and she went around the back of the house, Bruce was standing there holding a weed eater, and he chased me around the yard with it completely destroying the backs of my ankles and the backs of my legs and all kinds of craziness. To this day, I still can't weed eat. I will let the yard grow up to six feet before I would weed eat."

When Casey's grandfather arrived home and saw what happened, he tended to her wounds and as Casey put it, "did everything he could to protect us and not let us get taken away by Child Protective Services – Mom being so far away, Bruce being right there, PawPaw so afraid CPS would take us out and away from all the situation, which they probably would have. So, I don't know exactly what happened. I just know the next day Bruce had lots of bashes and bruises on his body."

Friday of that week, Casey's grandfather didn't make it home before the bus arrived once again, but Bruce was nowhere in sight when the girls got home. Casey told her sister she would meet her at their grandparents' home after she gathered a few items of clothing so they could spend the night. When she opened the door, Bruce was waiting inside. He attacked her with a butcher knife nearly severing the main artery in her leg.

"Bruce was screaming at me the whole time telling me I was ruining his good name. I had two big cuts in the upper part of my leg near my private area because he said he was going to make sure nobody else wanted to be down there, and so I was bleeding everywhere," she said.

Luckily, Casey's grandfather pulled into the driveway shortly after the girls got off the bus and rushed to her aid. Her aunt happened to stop by and took her sister away before she saw what happened. Casey's grandfather took her to the emergency room and "told a big story about how I fell and hurt myself so that I wouldn't get taken away, and by the next weekend, Bruce had moved."

She still bears scars from the attack, and as she told me the story and quickly and very intentionally moved on, with this being the last she spoke of Bruce, I was distinctly aware that the scars on her leg weren't the only scars she carries from that day.

With the daily threat of abuse removed from her life, Casey moved on through her teen years without those dark shadows looming physically around her. As she grew into young adulthood, Casey did a great deal of "Daddy searching, I'll just be honest. Dated every wrong guy I could've ever dated." She went to college for two and a half years and dropped out to follow a boyfriend to Birmingham,

Alabama, before moving to Tallahassee, Florida, to live with her mother when the relationship with the boyfriend ended.

"That's where I met Doug," Casey said. "I was working part-time at a day care and met him at a smoothie shop next door. Knowing him was sort of like, 'Oh, I have somebody to talk to and somebody to get me out of my mom's house. I'm 20 years old. I'm not just hanging out with a drunk grown-up all the time.' I was never a drinker. I never drank. I never did any of that."

Doug came over to her mother's house to meet her family and to take Casey on a date. According to her, the date went well. They went out to eat, saw a movie, and he was "a complete gentleman, nice guy, perfect little Floridian boy that you can imagine, blond hair, blue eyes, beautiful from top to bottom. Here I am, little southern belle Casey who's, while gone through a lot, still semi-naïve about the ways of the world, so we decided to go out again."

A week later, Doug picked her up to take her to a bar. Casey had been to only one bar before that night with a friend whose boyfriend knew the owner and was able to sneak them in before they were 18 back in her home state. She didn't quite know what to expect when they arrived.

"So, we showed up, and it's like a party, nothing like this little girl has ever experienced," she said. "There's drinks flying, and there's girls dressed half-naked, and all this crazy stuff. I was just completely overwhelmed, and Doug knew that. He even asked me if I was uncomfortable, and I told him I wasn't, even though I was *completely* uncomfortable. He said, 'Okay, we have this table we always get.' Come to find out, it's the manager's table, so you get all the special treatment. I quickly started to realize he's been here before."

Casey explained to Doug once again that she preferred not to drink to excess and rarely ever drank. He knew Casey's feelings about drinking because of her mother's alcoholism. She asked for an energy drink mixed with light vodka and began sipping on it trying to pace herself and acclimate to the party environment.

"We're all having fun," she said, "and as the night goes on, I start realizing I'm looser than I normally am, and I'm louder than I normally am, and things just kind of get foggy. I'm not really sure about what's going on. I told Doug, 'I'm not feeling well. Something's wrong. I'm having a bad reaction, and I'm not even drinking very much.' He said, 'No, you're just having fun. This is what happens.'

"Come to find out later on, he was getting them to add more alcohol to my drink than I thought. My drink never got empty. He was continually adding vodka to it. Somebody later told me they thought he possibly put GHB[3] in it, too."

She sat down and tried to relax but still felt like something wasn't right. She continued telling Doug she didn't feel well and finally talked him into taking her home.

---

[3] GHB (gamma-hydroxybutyrate) is a drug commonly known to be used as a date rape drug for its ability to induce unconsciousness and memory loss in people who take it without knowing.

"He said he would take me back to my mom's house since it wasn't that far away," she said. "We got in the car, and I passed out. When I woke up, we were somewhere at some house that I had no idea where we were. I was naked from the waist down, and I heard water running. I kind of rolled over, and I just remember hurting so bad. My stomach hurt. Everything hurt. All my private areas hurt. My boobs hurt. I had had sex before voluntarily and knew that was not the way things felt. I started to roll over and get up and realized I didn't have clothes on. That was when panic started to set in, and I hollered out for him."

Casey said Doug came out and stood "there in all his Florida sun-beamed glory with a towel around his waist, and I said, 'I thought you were taking me home,' and he said, 'No, you don't remember in the car you wanted to come home with me?' I was like, 'I don't remember that, and I find it hard to believe I would've said that.' I was never a sleep-with-someone-on-the-first-date or even the sec-ond date – *maybe* the six-month date! – kind of girl. Nothing made sense. I kept trying to explain to him that couldn't be right. He kept saying, 'Yeah, Casey. Yeah, Casey. Don't you remember?' I said, 'I know I didn't drink that much. I don't drink.' He said, 'Well, that's what you said. This is what happened.'"

Casey was scared. She asked Doug to take her to her mother's house. She got dressed as quickly as she could and tried to piece together what happened between the bar and when she woke up. When she got home, she struggled to focus. She said her brain didn't feel right, and she didn't go to work. She took a shower and slept most of the day.

Later that night, she woke up screaming hysterically. Phyllis ran into the room demanding, "What's going on?!"

Casey yelled, "He raped me! He raped me! I just realized he raped me!"

Phyllis looked at her in shock and asked, "What are you talking about?"

Casey told her, "Last night when I didn't come home, it was because he raped me. He brought me to his house when I told him to bring me to your house."

Phyllis questioned Casey about the events of the night before with disbelief and no attempt to comfort her daughter.

"Are you sure?" Phyllis asked skeptically. "Sometimes whenever you're drinking you say things you may not mean, and guys take it the wrong way."

Casey was adamant.

"No! *I know!* I know that I *didn't* want to do that."

Casey said her mother continued questioning her relentlessly, and nothing Casey said deterred her.

"There was nothing I could say to make her believe me," she said. "It was all my fault. I shouldn't have done it. I shouldn't have put myself in that situation. I shouldn't have said anything sexual to him. I don't think I even did, and, if I did, I don't have any recollection of it."

Later that day, Casey loaded everything she owned into her car and began the long drive back to her hometown and back to her PawPaw, her "angel." She called him after she got on the road crying desperate tears that had been building since she was a young girl, tears that begged to know what to do and how to deal with a mother who had told her she was raped because she asked for it. When she explained what happened, he simply said, "Come home."

"I drove straight back," Casey said. "I didn't stop to use the bathroom. I didn't stop to do anything. I was petrified of everything. I remember that ride so well. If I got boxed in by 18-wheelers, I started having a panic attack. That's when I started getting lost. I started questioning, 'Why me? Why did my father leave me when I was a kid to endure all this Hell I've endured? Why does my mother just not care and doesn't want to believe anything I say? What's wrong with me? What did I do to deserve this?'

"And even some resentment. There was some resentment I held toward my little sister because her life is peachy keen, and she didn't have all these fears because I protected her, and then she walked around with a chip on her shoulder because my grandfather took care of me, and she would always say, 'You're PawPaw's favorite.'"

While moving home may have brought relief from living with Phyllis and seeing Doug around town, Casey quickly discovered that her grandfather's rules were strict. It wasn't too long after moving home that she moved out and began working at a local restaurant that required her to wear a skimpy uniform and flirt with the patrons, both male and female.

"Along with that came the atmosphere of drugs, guys, and everything, and due to my lack of willpower and the state I was in in my life, I jumped in headfirst," Casey said. "If you wanted to give it to me, I would try it. At that point, it was, 'What do I have to lose? I don't have anybody really, and my grandfather isn't going to find out about this stuff, so I'm living on my own and paying my own bills and if I have the extra money, sure.' I started doing cocaine, smoking pot a lot, and took pills a few times, but that was nothing."

That unfortunate turn led Casey down what she calls "The Road to Redemption."

"I went through four years of pure Hell. There were all these guys coming in and out and around. I left the restaurant and was working for a lawyer making decent money as a single person, had a nice apartment in a great part of town, and I thought, 'For once in my life, things are going my way, and I'm having fun.' Then the drugs got me. One night, Phyllis and I hadn't been speaking for a long time after she told me she would rather see me dead than pour out the glass of whiskey in her hand.

"Something happened that night, I don't even remember what, and I did too much. I remember waking up the next morning. I had already been in therapy, and my therapist – I'll never forget him, my second angel – for whatever reason, he said he woke up that morning and thought, 'I need to check on Casey,' and I didn't answer. He called again, and I didn't answer. He called my office, and my boss said I wasn't there. He came to my house and found me. I don't remember any of it. Everybody thought that I was trying to commit suicide. I wasn't. I just did too much, and maybe subconsciously I was (trying to commit suicide). Who knows? At that point, I had nothing."

Casey woke up to an emergency medical team taking her down the stairs and saw her boss and therapist standing outside.

"I was so confused. That's all I can remember being. Nothing made sense. Later, I found out my blood sugar was 14. At that point, my boss, my therapist, and my grandfather got together while I was on 72-hour hold in the hospital and said that I would go to rehab. I left straight from the hospital in the most embarrassing way in the back seat of a police car hauled over to the rehab facility where I stayed for seven days. I only had to stay for three but volunteered for four more. From there, I went to another inpatient facility for two more weeks and got completely clean and sober. Everything in my life changed."

Her grandfather refused to allow Phyllis near Casey anymore. According to Casey, Phyllis had become, and still is, very verbally abusive. Her grandfather wouldn't allow Phyllis at family events if Casey planned to be there, and if anyone mentioned Bruce's name, "He would lose it. PawPaw would say, 'That man's name is not to be spoken in this house. You don't talk about him. I'm the reason he doesn't live here anymore. I ran him off.'"

As hard as it was to be unable to reconcile with Phyllis and share a fairy tale moment where her mother turned away from alcohol and chose her daughter over a drink, Casey was realistic. She said she has never known her mother to be anything other than an alcoholic, and as her grandfather always told her, "Casey, your best friends are your paycheck and your mama, and you got the raw end of the deal on the mama part, so your best dependence is on that paycheck."

So that's how she moved forward, focusing on her job, her "best friend" the paycheck, and on pulling herself together. When she finally started getting her feet on the ground and making a way for herself, she met Ross.

"I bought a Mustang from him at a car lot and ended up having his baby," she said with a laugh, although I quickly learned that would be one of the few moments she would share anything light-hearted about Ross.

"That relationship, while there was no abuse physically or sexually, was the most tumultuous relationship ever. He was addicted to sex. Coming from where I came from where sex was almost always evil to me, it would end up in knock-down, drag-out screaming fights at 2 a.m. How we ended up with a baby is a miracle to me as much as we fought about it because he was of the opinion that if you're going to get together and you're planning to marry, you're going to be a wife and that means you do it every night. That's part of your duty. He never forced me to do anything, but there were lots of moments I was wishing I was somewhere else."

I asked if he knew her history of abuse, and, if so, did that make their sexual relationship feel coerced on the nights when she wished she were somewhere else and participated as part of her "duty."

"Oh yeah," she said. "He knew the whole rehab story, and he would still try to get me to drink, to loosen me up and get me to do things he wanted me to do. Even to this day, I don't drink that much. It's just not something I do."

Because of her history of sexual abuse from such a young age, Casey has always been open with her gynecologist about what took place with Bruce and Josh. Testing showed that her uterus was tilted due to the damage sustained through years of molestation at a young age, and several of her pelvic bones "were malformed due to continuous pounding when they're supposed to be growing properly. They said I probably wouldn't be able to have children of my own. In fact, I dated a great guy for several years, and we never used protection and never even had a scare. It wasn't a concern."

Casey said she pinpointed the night she got pregnant with her daughter, and it was a night that Ross coerced her into sex.

She doesn't let that change how she views her pregnancy.

"I choose to block that out because out of that came the very best thing that ever happened to me. The morning I took the test, I took five tests because I didn't believe it. That instant, I remember thinking, 'I'm done. I will never allow my daughter to think it's okay to treat a woman the way her daddy treated me. I will never let her think she's not in a safe and secure environment.' That was never a safe and secure environment for me, so how could I make it that way for her? At that moment…"

She paused, wiped her eyes, tried to hold back tears.

"I'm trying not to cry," she said. I assured her a few tears – or all the tears she could spare – were quite okay, especially considering all she was sharing and the fact that now was the first time she had paused to let emotion catch her.

She continued, "That was the ultimate life-changing, most healing moment for me because at that moment, I realized, 'I have somebody else now who depends on me,' and in my own little twisted mind, God put her there for that reason because He knew I was alone. I've always said, 'Savannah, you're my little ray of sunshine because if it weren't for you, I don't know where I would be.'"

After finding out she was pregnant, Casey saw her life change dramatically. She changed the way she lived, the way she acted, the way she felt as a person. From the inside out, she was living for the first time with purpose.

"I just knew deep down in my soul I never wanted her to experience any of the things I experienced growing up – the alcoholism, the abuse, every bit of it. Ross will never grow up. I've learned to understand and accept that."

While she was pregnant with Savannah, though, Casey was still trying to create a family life with Ross. She said she prayed and attempted to force a relationship so her child did not have to grow up in a home without both parents present.

"I fought it, and I fought it, and I fought it until I was exhausted, and I would call my grandfather and say, 'I can't fight anymore. I don't know what to do. What am I doing wrong that makes him not want me, that makes him not want this family?'"

That's when her grandfather would always give her the advice about her best friends being her paycheck and her mama and how she got a raw deal on her mama. At that point in her life, he added words Casey needed to hear, "You can't put your stock and your happiness in *him*. He isn't going to make you happy."

After she spoke with her grandfather, Casey said she began to notice things in Ross she hadn't seen before and realize he wasn't the man she thought she loved. However, her stubborn need to hold on and make the relationship work was difficult to overcome because living with Ross felt like her "first, real-life, grown-up relationship. We were bringing a child into the world," she said.

When Ross didn't come home one night, Casey awoke to hear him coming in the following morning at 6 a.m. With a still-foggy, trying-to-wake-up brain, her initial thought was, "Was he outside feeding the dogs this early?" At that point, she noticed he was wearing the same clothes from the day before. When she asked where he had been, he claimed to have fallen asleep the night before after pulling into an inlet on the side of the road to avoid a charge for driving while intoxicated.

"Stupid me wanted to believe every word he was telling me because I wanted my family to be together," Casey said. The following night, she called her best friend Grant to pick her up and follow Ross to see where he was really going, and they discovered him at his ex-wife's house. After two hours of waiting for him to leave, Casey gave up.

She told Grant, "Apparently, he's going to spend the night again, so you can just bring me home."

They stopped to get something to eat, and by the time they arrived at the house, Ross was already there. Ross and Grant had never gotten along, and Ross "became unhinged because he had been drinking. He started telling me how I was going to be nothing but my mother and that there was no way he would let me have custody of my child. It got so super, super ugly – uglier than I've ever seen Grant. He has a hot head, but it takes a lot to lead him there. Ross said he would never stop sleeping with his ex-wife because I would 'never be as good of a lay as she is,' and Grant just cold-cocked him."

Ross threatened to call the police. Largely pregnant and stressed, Casey grabbed a few clothes and went to stay with Grant. The following weekend, she retrieved what she could of her belongings and has maintained a civil but strained relationship with Ross ever since.

"I decided at that moment that it was me and Savannah to the end, and that was going to be our life," Casey said.

With her rocky journey beginning to smooth out and her infant daughter by her side, Casey was finally breathing more easily and enjoying a quiet, semi-peaceful life. Her boss who had stood by her side during rehab was still her employer and was mentoring her not only at work but through life in general. Savannah was healthy and happy, and being single was a welcome option.

"Then, out of nowhere, swooped in Jay with his superhero cape," Casey said. "I said the night I met him that I would end up marrying him. Our first date he came over and hung out after Savannah went to bed. He didn't meet her until she was six months old. I made sure of it. I didn't have a babysitter, and she wasn't staying with my drunk mom. I was a single mom on one salary with a deadbeat baby daddy. Our date consisted of watching reality TV on my couch."

Jay's family embraced both Casey and Savannah wholeheartedly. Now married with two more daughters, Casey is settled into a happy, well-adjusted life with a man who respects her and understands her need to break the cycle of distrust and abuse. Jay treats Savannah as if she is biologically his own, and their bond is strong. Savannah still sees her biological father regularly but is aware of his on-again, off-again problems with drinking and has a surface-level knowledge of the history of issues between her parents. As Savannah matures, Casey said she will share with her what she needs or wants to know, as appropriate, both about her tumultuous relationship with Ross and about the broken, painful road that ultimately led her to him.

"Will you speak differently to your other daughters about your past and about the things they need to know about the world than you will to Savannah?" I asked.

Casey paused, looking around for answers, narrowing her eyes and looking in front of her as if she were midair editing her truths about to be shared. The uneasy reality seemed to be something she had pondered but perhaps not quite yet decided how to address.

Having three daughters of my own with the eldest's being from a previous relationship that didn't end well, I understand the dilemma. You want to share equitably with all three, but the child who experienced different things in her early life and has biological ties to someone who caused both of you pain – and will someday require difficult explanations – is the one who may receive differently biased lessons.

It's challenging to describe why this feels necessary. It just does.

"I do think I will speak differently to them," she finally said, "but a lot about the same things," and she left it at that. I didn't press for more, as it was clear she had not truly yet determined exactly how that will look in her family.

"How do you think the things you have been through affect your parenting style?" I asked.

"I'm not a helicopter mom," she replied. "I've made it my goal to not be that. I don't want my children where they think everything is where you just walk around with rose-colored glasses. I let my kids feel the disappointment and understand that you're not always going to win and that life doesn't always go your way. Sometimes you spend a lot of your life feeling like you got the raw end of the deal and that somebody owes you something, but, in reality, you're not owed anything.

"That's what I tell Savannah a lot as far as earning things and school stuff. There's nothing in this world that you're going to get just handed to you. You work for it, and great things happen. You make the right decisions. I've been very open and honest with her about alcoholism and drug abuse. Those things run rampant on both sides of her family, and I don't want her to go down that track."

After all she has lived through and put herself through as well – from being molested, abused, and abandoned in childhood and raped in early adulthood to a string of negative relationships, drug addiction, numb years of mental and emotional torment to more than two decades of seeking a replacement father – Casey has maintained a positive, work-hard, pray-hard, nobody-owes-you-anything attitude that she tries to pass along to her daughters. Not everyone rises with such an impressively constructive outlook from the ashes of a life that burned in desperation for so many years.

So, I looked across at this positive, well-adjusted Southern lady with the sweet voice and the big smile, three intelligent, beautiful daughters, an affectionately dedicated soulmate, a successful career, and a love of God and faith that runs deeper than any wound can hurt her, and I asked the hard question, "If you came face-to-face with Bruce today, what would you do?"

This was one time she didn't hesitate.

"I would probably lose it in total anger finally being able to yell at him and get it all out," she replied.

"If he sat down right here, and you finally had a chance to say whatever you wanted to say to him, what would you say?" I asked.

Again, there was no hesitation as this woman I know to be of a kind, compassionate nature took a long breath and pulled the words from deep within herself in a genuinely unwavering place as she replied, "I would say, 'I hope with everything I believe in God and in my religion that the Hell you're going to endure is exponentially more than the Hell I've had to endure for 36 years because I think you deserve it.' I would also tell him he doesn't realize the ways he impacted not only my life and his kids' lives but also my family's life and all the people around me who are now extra careful and extra observant when maybe that's a good thing to be that way, but maybe they shouldn't have *had* to be that way. I would tell him that honestly whatever pain and horror that is inflicted on him is what is meant to be."

"What would you say if he apologized?" I asked.

She rolled her eyes. Grunted. Exhaled in exasperation.

"I would tell him the same thing I told Josh when he tried to say that to me," she said. "I would say, 'I accept your apology, but at the same time, it doesn't really hold a lot of water with me. What you did is engrained in my soul now, and there is nothing you could ever be able to do that would make me think differently of you. You are always going to be scum to me, somebody that I wouldn't spit on if you were on fire.'

"The same goes for Josh, especially for him and knowing he was repeating the cycle. That was my big thing with Jay when we got married. I wanted to break the cycle of abuse. I wanted to break the cycle of alcoholism. We have family members who were involved in both those things. That's my goal in life. I think that's why God decided to give me children when everything was stacked against me to have kids, and I'm here to break that cycle. I'm here to show my kids you *can* grow up in a world where there are terrible people, and you don't know who they are. They could be standing right outside that door, but there are also *great* people in this world."

Despite the stories captured in this book, the undeniable truth is that there are countless people in this world who are fantastically great. I was honored to sit across from one for nearly two hours hearing her stories of surviving childhood trauma at the hands of a heartless stepfather and an absent, alcoholic mother and putting herself through years of searching and physical abuse trying to fill mental and emotional gaps.

As we continued talking in the days after the interview, she shared that her faith in God and the power of His hand in her life were being restored to unprecedented levels. I shared with her in one of our conversations that, in my strong-willed independence, I had always felt the pull and urgency of Bible verses such as Philippians 4:13, which says, "I can do all things through Christ who strengthens me." I was a stubborn person who thought all my damaged flaws and problems were mine to fix, and through God's help, I was going to be the one to fix everything wrong with myself and the world around me and that, with enough of a take-charge attitude, that was exactly what I could accomplish. I would be the driver, and God would be riding strong in the sidecar as I drove proudly across the finish line to victory.

What I learned through the process of healing, though, and what I shared with Casey, is that what I really need to always focus on, and what she needed to focus on – and what so many people need to focus on regardless of what they have been hurt by or where they are in life – is Psalm 46:10 – "Be still, and know that I am God." By allowing peace and stillness to settle in, by allowing the problems of her past to catch up to her, and by knowing that God was going to be her shepherd through the hard times and guide her through the pain, Casey was able to be still, to stand in the midst of her turmoil for a moment, and to say, "I am more."

Whether she still feels the same negativity toward Bruce and wishes the everlasting, painful purgatory on him that she did on the day of our interview, I have no idea. We haven't spoken of it, and I won't ask her about it again. Casey is in a good place. Her family is in a good place. She has spoken about her trauma in its full details for the first time to her husband, to her mother-in-law, to her pastor, and, now, to the world.

And she can say out loud *and* in her heart and mean it when she says, "I am more." Her grandfather passed away years ago, but if he were here today to see the woman and mother she has become, I know he would surely say, "You always were."

"There was nothing I could say to make her believe me," she said. "It was all my fault. I shouldn't have done it. I shouldn't have put myself in that situation. I shouldn't have said anything sexual to him. I don't think I even did, and, if I did, I don't have any recollection of it."

Chapter Thirteen

Elisa

"He never should have been there. I knew he shouldn't be there…"

Elisa was uncertain about sharing her story and initially declined. Prior to our interview, she had told only minimal details to a few close family members. In fact, she held onto her painful secret for nearly nine years before the first time she broke down and told anyone.

Despite her nine-year, self-imposed silence, the details of what happened to Elisa were anything but quiet in her memories. Almost as soon as she entered the interview room, she began fumbling for words and trying to explain. Before I could get out so much as a simple greeting and thank her for reconsidering talking to me, she began speaking hurriedly, almost rambling, as if she had rehearsed each word individually to make sure she could say them out loud.

"I know I have to share responsibility in what happened. Please understand. I'm not without fault. I get that. I totally do," Elisa said, gazing past me as if she were reading a cue card positioned over my right shoulder, "and I know when you write this, my part in all of it will be clear. There isn't a day – or like even a minute really, you know? – I don't wish I would've at least *tried* to handle things differently. I did the only thing I knew to do when things were happening so fast, but still. I guess what they say about hindsight being 20/20 is true, huh?"

She perched apprehensively on the edge of the hunter green hardback chair, tapped her foot while she talked, and rested both of her hands on the table as if she needed to steady herself. With her straightforward, clearly rehearsed opening statement out in the open, she heaved a deep sigh, pushed herself slowly to the back of the chair, and made uneasy eye contact with me. I attempted to reassure her with an understandingly kind smile. She seemed to relax a little but still sat tensely and crossed her arms protectively in front of her. It was difficult to decide if she had retreated into defense mode or was giving herself a hug of reassurance.

"Thank you for sharing that," I told her. "I'm sorry you feel like what happened to you was in some way your fault, but you're free to feel however you choose to feel. We all are. My goal with this book is to share your story and the stories of others and to help each of you tell how you moved on after your assault so others can learn from how you coped and how you've grown. The best way we can help others is to share our stories. By talking about it, maybe we can prevent others from becoming victims in the first place. Thank you for being willing to share. I know it isn't easy."

Her face softened slightly around the edges as we began getting to know each other and sharing our backgrounds and our current paths in life. Eventually, her arms unfolded, she leaned forward, and her tone relaxed. After chatting casually for a while, though, a resolute look swept across her face, she looked down at the table, and she changed the topic back to what originally brought us together – her own assault at the hands of her ex-boyfriend.

"Thank you for giving me time to warm up, but you don't have to beat around the bush," Elisa said, refocusing our conversation. "I'm not nervous anymore."

Indeed, she wasn't. She began telling me about her assault without my having to ask questions or define how I hoped the conversation might flow. She talked for nearly an hour relating background information about her relationship with the man who assaulted her, what had taken place since the assault, and so many other things that are not found in this book, all of which were important but could easily be a book of their own, which I encouraged her to consider.

Her story was frustrating. I found myself wanting to go back in time and warn her not to let him in, to stand outside her home and yell, "Tell him, 'No!'" at just the right time, or to break down the door and help her, but as she reminded me several times as she spoke, "You can't look back. What's done is done. You can only heal and move on." She said it so many times, in fact, I wondered if she believed it or if she were still trying to convince herself. Like many of us, the truth on that particular statement is probably somewhere in the middle and always will be.

Also, like many sexual assault survivors, Elisa recalls her assault as if it happened yesterday. The way his voice changed from soft and persuasive to stern and demanding when she told him, "No," the way his dark eyes narrowed to a squint when he threatened her, how her heart beat faster when he mentioned what he would do to their son, Daniel, if she didn't do what he wanted – so many still-haunting details.

"Ben and I hadn't spoken in several months," she said. "Our breakup was ugly, loud. I think any time there's a kid involved, it gets that way and gets heated really fast. Unfortunately, he was really threatening toward me and Daniel, and the police had to be called several times. He threatened to kill all three of us. He kept saying he was going to crash his car through my bedroom window so he could take all three of us out at once and we could go out of this world together."

Elisa said that for a while when Ben was making threats, she and Daniel, who was a baby at the time, slept in different rooms nearly every night but never in the bedroom that faced the road. Ben followed her all over town, called relentlessly at all hours, and sat in her driveway with the lights shining into her bedroom windows. He began showing up drunk in the wee hours of the morning and ringing the doorbell for several minutes at a time while banging on the door and yelling for her to open it. Too afraid of what would happen if she opened the door, Elisa refused, and the continuously ringing doorbell and pounding on the door woke up Daniel each time.

Elisa told me that when this happened, all she could do was hold her baby and reassure him as much as she could, but there was only so much she could do to combat the noise. She was too scared to call the police for fear they wouldn't do anything except tell him to leave since he hadn't actually harmed her or their son. She knew him well enough to know that, after the police were gone, he would come back and follow through on his threats.

"After a while, it was more than we could take. I didn't realize I had more power than I thought. Because of the hundreds of phone calls and the way he stalked me around town and came to the house, I eventually was able to get a protective order for harassment," she said. "The judge issued a one-year, 100-yard protective order that covered both me and Daniel. A month later, he was back calling me again, and they put him in jail for violating the order. It's just a piece of paper after all. If he wanted to walk right through it, there was nothing I could do unless the police chose to enforce it. Thank the Good Lord above, our officers listened and were willing to help."

A few months later in January, Ben was out and attempting to adjust to a normal life. He moved in with his mother and was, according to mutual friends, doing much better. He was working a steady job and maintaining a more positive lifestyle with better choices and influences. Elisa said he was respecting the protective order and keeping his distance. She stayed in touch with his mother, who happily reported noticeable changes in him and stated that she thought the time away to clear his head while he was in jail had served him well.

Living in a relatively small town, though, it was difficult to avoid running into each other. Elisa said she pulled up at a gas station on a cold afternoon in mid-January without immediately realizing the car next to her was Ben's. He moved to stop his transaction and leave, but she motioned for him to finish without worry. According to the terms of the protective order, Ben could not be within 100 yards of her for one year, and they were instructed on the record by the judge that it was not her responsibility to leave – it was his. Despite that, Elisa thought this minor encounter could be managed without incident.

"I didn't think it was that big of a deal. He was doing such a good job with all the changes he had made. I could see the frustration on his face when I pulled up behind him," she said. "It didn't seem right to make him stop pumping gas and go somewhere else just because I pulled up. I thought, 'Surely we can at least get gas in the same place, right?'"

He kept his back to her, and the longer they stood there, the more Elisa's guard came down. She said she stood there watching him and thinking how differently he was handling himself and how much more respectfully he was treating her than he had just a few months earlier.

"I went over to him and asked if he wanted to know how Daniel was doing," Elisa said. "His face lit up. Now, I think it was probably because I was talking to him, but, at the time, I stupidly thought it was because he was happy to hear news about his son."

Before she knew what she was saying, and even though there was a protective order in place, Elisa told Ben if he wanted to stop by the house the next night to see Daniel, he could.

"I told him he had to arrive on time and be gone right after dinner. He had to act right and follow my rules, the visit was about

Daniel, and if he stepped one step out of line, I was going to call 9-1-1 so fast his head was going to spin right off his shoulders."

Ben agreed and the following night showed up promptly at 6:30 p.m. nicely dressed and with the happiest smile Elisa had seen in quite some time. The visit went well, and Elisa told him she would consider allowing him to see Daniel on a somewhat regular schedule if he could continue proving himself to be a changed man. He left that evening exactly as he had agreed to and never crossed any lines, much to Elisa's surprise.

"I swear I didn't even know this person who showed up at my house," Elisa told me. "He was a changed man. There was definitely no chance for reconciliation, of course, but I was so, so happy for Daniel. I'd moved on with Will, a man I loved very much. We're married now, and Daniel already thought of him as a father even back then. But Daniel deserved a chance to know his biological father, and I kept hoping Ben would get himself together for his son's sake."

Elisa shared what had taken place during the visit with Will, and even knowing how Ben had acted several months earlier, they agreed that if Ben could continue proving he had changed, occasional visits with Daniel could be allowed. When Elisa called Ben to tell him he could come visit Daniel again the following week, he thanked her.

"He was so friendly, so kind," she said. "He really seemed to be on such an awesome path. I had high hopes this would be his big turnaround."

The following week when Ben came to the house to visit Daniel was one of the coldest nights of the winter with record lows predicted throughout the region. As Ben played with Daniel, Elisa asked how the living arrangements were working out with Ben's mom. Their relationship had always been strained at best when they lived together, but from what they had both said, things appeared to be going well.

"He told me they'd had a big blow-up that morning about him coming in late. She told him not to come back until he could respect her house and her rules," Elisa said. "When I asked where he was staying, he said he was going to sleep in his car and try to talk some sense into her the next day."

Knowing the temperatures were supposed to drop into the mid-teens that night, Elisa said she fought with herself about what to do. She excused herself to go to the bathroom and texted his mom to see if Ben's story was valid. The reply came back that they did have an argument and that he was not welcome in her home until they could work through some things.

"I didn't know what to do. Here he was in my home playing with our son, and it was freezing cold outside. Unless he left his car running all night, which he couldn't afford to do because gas prices were so ridiculous, he could've frozen to death trying to sleep in his car, and I knew he didn't have money for a hotel. He'd lost all the friends he used to have when he tried to straighten out his life and get away from people who smoked weed and partied all the time," she said.

Elisa said she didn't have money to give him for a hotel and needed what she had to buy groceries and pay day care. She knew he wouldn't go to a local shelter based on experiences he had there when his mother kicked him out of their home when he was a teenager.

"I was fighting with myself so hard. If I had to do it over again, I would tell him right then when he first brought up the problems with his mom that he should go home and work it out with her. Be a man. Fix your problems. Sorry for you, but it's not my fault and not my problem to fix."

What she did instead, though, was let her guard down and tell this man against whom the courts had issued a protective order for both her and her son that he could stay in their home on the couch for one night only so he didn't have to sleep in his car in freezing temperatures.

"I gave him a pillow and a blanket and took Daniel with me to the bedroom," she said. I could tell we were approaching a stressful part of her story by how she perched apprehensively on the edge of her chair once again and tapped her foot. "Pretty soon, he was knocking on the bedroom door asking if he could lie on the bed next to Daniel like he used to when he was first born and watch him drift off to sleep."

And there it was – that deep, closed-eyes sigh I became oh-so-familiar with as I talked to survivors. That sigh that lets them regain their composure, center themselves, and take their brains to a less stressful place. I like to refer to it as "finding my Jesus," but another survivor called it "calming the stabs." Yet another told me she didn't realize she did it. When I asked about it, Elisa said, "Sometimes I have to stop and breathe so I don't cry. It's still hard. Talking about it feels like I'm in it. In my mind, I still feel like I walk around in it a lot."

I asked her to continue and apologized for interrupting. She deeply sighed once more and retreated back into her moment before she said, "I told him, 'No,' but he seemed so sad, and he had been so nice. I really wanted him to connect with Daniel, so I let him lie down for just a minute while I was putting Daniel to bed. He was being so great, and it was this really loving moment. At one point, he said, 'Isn't this nice the three of us here together,' and I told him, 'It's nice for Daniel.' He knew what I meant and didn't push it. That seemed so sweet that he was respectful of me and my relationship with Will and didn't push. It wasn't like him to *not* push.

"Looking back – and trust me when I say that I've spent I don't know how many hundreds of hours looking back – every word he said and every move he made was leading up to his big move. He wasn't being sweet. He was making sure my guard was down," Elisa said.

When Daniel was finally asleep, Ben asked if he could lie there and watch him for a while. Elisa told him he was pushing his luck and that he needed to return to the living room where they agreed he would sleep. Ben asked if he could stay in the room with them since it was warmer, and Elisa adamantly told him, "No." Ben reluctantly left after continuing to lie there for a few more minutes talking to her about Daniel, and Elisa said she quickly shut the door behind him as soon as he left.

"About five minutes later, the door creaked open. Unfortunately, the lock was broken, so he just let himself in," she said. "I asked what he wanted, but he didn't say anything. I had my back to the door, so I didn't see him coming around to my side of the bed until he was already there. He crouched down by me and looked up at me with those big ole pleading puppy dog eyes he always tried to manipulate me with when we were together and said, 'Come to the living room with me.' I couldn't believe what I was hearing. I didn't even answer him right away. I just laid there staring at him."

Elisa said it took a few seconds to get her wits about her enough to realize what he said before she replied.

"I said, 'Have you lost your ever-lovin' mind?' He said, 'Come on, Elisa! You know you still want me, too. You'll always want me. Come to the living room.' Of course, I refused and told him to get out of my bedroom. I honestly thought he was joking or must be high or something. He got so angry. He punched the floor, and said, 'Dammit, Elisa! Come to the living room.'"

When she refused and told him she would never go anywhere with him again, his demands escalated.

"He said, 'Come to the living room with me, or I'll wake up the baby.' I actually laughed. Out loud. I told him, 'Do you know how long it takes me to get that baby to sleep every night? Go ahead. I'm used to putting that kid to sleep, and you're still not going to get any.' That's when he threatened to shake Daniel. I was really nervous but tried not to let him see it. I sort of laughed and said, 'No. You won't.' His reply was, 'I'll shake him until he cries.' I was getting really scared, but I tried to blow it off like I wasn't and said, 'No. You really won't, but thanks for playing this little game. Now go back to the living room like I told you to. Please.'"

Elisa said that's when he got closer to the bed, put his face closer to hers, and said, "I'll shake you both until you cry."

She sat straight up in the bed, looked him directly in the eyes with sudden seriousness and an understanding of the significance of his words as she asked, "You'll do what?"

Elisa said he replied, "I'll shake you both until you *stop* crying."

She said her mind raced for a few brief seconds about possible alternatives to going with him to the living room to do what she knew he wanted her to do. Her neighbor who sometimes checked on her and her son worked in the oil field and was out of town, and the likelihood of the people in the home on the other side hearing her screams from the distance at which they lived was unlikely. Her phone was out of reach, and the only other person who would hear her pleas for help was her son, who couldn't help and would only get hurt if she fought.

"I stood up like he wanted me to. My head was spinning. I wasn't sure if I should walk or fall to my knees and cry and beg or what I should do. He grabbed both my hands in one of his hands, and started walking me down the long hallway in the dark to the living room like a prisoner," Elisa said, quietly, almost in a whisper. I could tell as she talked that the scene was playing out in mental images, just as it had every time she had thought of it for so many years.

"He stopped at my couch and didn't even speak to me," she said. "He pointed for me to lie down, and he pulled my shorts down. He didn't care about my shirt. He only needed the part of me that he needed, I guess. I turned my head toward the back of the couch so I didn't have to look at him, and it only took about three minutes, maybe less, of him on top of me for him to be done. I can still smell his hair – obviously he showered earlier that day, and I remember his mother always used a cheap, flowery-smelling shampoo. That mixed with cigarette smoke was heavy in his hair while he was leaning over me, and I can still smell it sometimes. Any time someone passes me with that smell on them, it's like being back on that couch again. When he was done, he didn't say anything. He just got up, pulled up his jeans and left them unzipped. He walked over to the sliding glass door on my patio and pulled it open a few inches so he could have a cigarette without going out in the cold."

Elisa said she didn't waste any time getting up from the couch.

"All I said to him was, 'Tomorrow morning, I want you to leave as soon as the alarm goes off. I have an early meeting.' He sort of nodded, gave me a thumbs up over his shoulder without turning around, and that was that. I didn't want to say anything to make him mad, so I just got up and went to the back of the house as fast as I could without making it look like I was trying to get away."

She went to her bedroom, shut the door behind her once again, and showered until the hot water ran out.

"I got Daniel out of the bed and put him in his bouncy seat in the bathroom floor," she said. "I locked the bathroom door behind me so we were behind at least one safe door. By the absolute grace of God, somehow that sweet, light-sleeping baby stayed asleep while I cried more tears in one night than I'd cried in several years put together, even during our breakup. It felt like my tears filled the shower just as much as the water coming from the faucet, and it was hard to tell which was which. I must've been trying to shower off every inch of my skin. I washed my hair, cut my fingernails. I even brushed my teeth, even though he didn't kiss me or make me do anything to him. Ben could have been out there stealing everything I owned. I didn't care. As long as he wasn't touching me anymore or hurting my son, I didn't care what he did."

Elisa didn't tell anyone what happened that night for many years. She was afraid of losing Will and felt the whole incident was her fault for allowing Ben into the house when there was a protective order intended to keep him away. She said she was ashamed that she had given up when her fear intensified beyond a point where she knew how to handle the situation.

"I should have fought him off or at least tried to," she said. "I feel like I rolled over and played dead out of sheer fear. I could have lost my boyfriend, who is now my husband, over my inability to tell this man, 'No.' He didn't deserve any part of me. I already had the best part of him lying in the bed sleeping soundly. I should have cut ties with Ben long before that night and moved on without looking back, but I had this romanticized notion of how people change and how they can be the people you need them to be. That's not true, or at least it isn't for him. He didn't deserve the chance to do that to me, and I'm the one who opened the door – *literally*. I know it's what they call 'coerced consent,' but I know any jury would've said he shouldn't have been there in the first place. That's just how these things work. This isn't a TV show. This is real life."

Clearly, Elisa is still psychologically hurting about the assault. She was tense as she told her story, but she glowed when she talked about Daniel and how he has developed into a smart, gentle-hearted, animal-loving, compassionate young man who loves his church, video games, art, music, and spending time with family and friends. He suffers from occasional anxiety problems that Elisa can't help but wonder might be attributable to nights of being held and con-soled while Ben caused chaos outside their home, as well as her ongoing stress at that time. Children are, after all, very perceptive, no matter how much we attempt to disguise our emotions.

According to Elisa, Ben left the following morning, just as she requested. Later that day, she texted him to say he couldn't come over for visits anymore.

"I told him we had to go back to not talking and to the way things were before with the protective order," she said. "He was furious. I told him if he texted me again, I would call the police and show them the texts."

Ben didn't contact her for a while at first, as she asked, but a couple of weeks later, he was in jail again for violating the protec-tive order. During court, the judge called Elisa to the front to educate her about how protective orders work.

"He was strict with me, just like he was with Ben," she said. "He reminded me that I can't decide on my own to let him come over. I don't get to decide the order isn't in place anymore. Ben told them how I had let him come over to my house in the hopes they'd cut him some slack, but it didn't work."

With Ben in jail for six months, Elisa worked with her attorney to continue the custody agreement proceedings that had already begun prior to his incarceration. She visited her attorney and asked him to speed up the process and requested that the protective order become permanent. When the attorney asked why there was a sudden urgency, it was the closest Elisa came during that time to revealing what happened.

"All I said was that I finally realized he was never going to stop, no matter how much he supposedly changed," she said. "Being a victims' rights attorney, I guess he knew enough about how these things usually play out to not press me on details. He told me if I ever wanted to talk about it or had something that needed to have legal action pursued against it, to let him know. I just looked back at him across the desk, kind of like I've been looking at you, I guess, all serious and stuff, and told him I was done being afraid. I also told him I would never agree to unsupervised visits with my son, and he agreed that shouldn't be a problem because of Ben's repeated violations of the protective order."

A few months later, the custody hearing was held, and Ben didn't show up. The judge signed the custody agreement making the protective order permanent and extending it to 1,500 feet. Daniel's supervised visits with Ben continued until right after he turned 3 when Ben abruptly terminated the visits and moved out-of-state to avoid prosecution on unrelated charges. He never reached out again, but Elisa said she still looks over her shoulder everywhere she goes.

"I don't think I'll ever stop looking for him," she said. "My son is getting ready to go to college now and able to take care of himself, but I still make sure the car door is locked as soon as we get in. If I go to the back to get something when we're both in the car, I lock the door when I get out and unlock it again when I get to the back out of fear that Ben might be lurking nearby. This man has lived several states away for years, and I still look for him everywhere I go. I jump every time I see a car like he used to have, and he doesn't even have a car like that anymore."

Elisa thanked me for giving her the chance to tell her story. I thanked her for trusting me to bring her story to life in a way that might help people understand the struggle someone goes through when their assault is the result of coerced consent.

"It's the worst," she said. "Every day, I live with the questions of 'What if I had fought him' and 'What if I had screamed for help' and 'Could this have ended differently?' I have to believe the different ending would have been the one he wrote that ended with me and Daniel being shaken until we stopped crying. I'd rather live with a lifetime of questions and anxiety than die trying to save myself from it."

Elisa's words will probably haunt me as much as her assault haunts her. Many of her questions and what-ifs are so similar to my thoughts after my own assault, and our interview was emotionally tiring for me on a level I didn't understand until it was over. Since we met, I have many times pondered the statement, "I'd rather live with a lifetime of questions and anxiety than die trying to save myself from it."

So many survivors probably feel the same way, but Elisa so perfectly put into words the paralyzing feeling we feel when we don't fight back. We want to fight. We want to run. We want to scream, to kick, to bite, to get away, to do *something, anything.*

But we don't.

We are paralyzed by fear, shame, uncertainty, surprise, guilt, whatever it might be for each person as their assault is taking place. We didn't fight back, and we all too often become the people society looks down on and questions whether we were victims or participants who later had regrets.

Elisa was a victim.

Yes, she consented, but it was coerced out of a fear for her life and for the life of her son. She did not want to be there. She would rather have been anywhere else in the three minutes or so her head faced the back of that couch. She would rather have been anywhere else each time in the years since then as she outwardly smiled all the while screaming internally as the memories of that night played out in alternate ways, some of which had violent endings she hoped would bring an even bigger smile to her as she pondered them but ultimately just took her to a place of sadness and prayer.

Elisa said she feels bad for all the "shameful things I thought of doing to him. I know he had a really abusive childhood, but you can't hurt other people because of things that were done to you. I pray for him now. I pray for myself. I pray for forgiveness for all the horribly terrible things I thought after that night, even though I meant them at the time. Sometimes I think I still do, but I try to pray right on through it. It's hard. It really is. I believe God sent him to my life to bring Daniel to me, and I'm grateful. I try to remember that and be thankful, but you know how old wounds are. They may heal, but those scars are always there."

Indeed, my new friend, I do.

Those wounds can often heal with time and prayer, but they can also leave scars to remind us of where we've been. For Elisa, she has Daniel to remind her that beautiful things can emerge from dark times in our lives, but those scars can also remind us of how far we've come on the God-blessed broken roads of life.

I pray, too, Elisa, for my assaulter, and now for your assaulter as well, and I pray for you and your son. I pray we all remember those among us who live with questions left behind by the pain of coerced consent that they may find peace in their hearts, in their minds, and in how they feel about those aching scars left behind by the trauma of sexual assault.

You *are* a victim.

You *are* strong.

You did what you thought was *right*.

You *survived*.

Keep taking those deep breaths and taking care of yourself and your son, and thank you for finding the courage to trust the world with your story.

"I know it's what they call 'coerced consent,' but I know any jury would've said he shouldn't have been there in the first place. That's just how these things work. This isn't a TV show. This is real life."

CHAPTER FOURTEEN

Lola

If you ever meet Lola, you won't guess anyone even dared to consider trying to dim her life's light. She has one of the happiest, eye-sparkling smiles and authentic, so-glad-to-know-you, never-meets-a-stranger personalities you'll ever see. She is fun, smart, witty, and has a love of people, volunteering, and her community that is tough to match.

It's difficult to imagine she has spent the majority of her life – since age 3, in fact – with the shadow of her stepfather looming over her. Until recently, he was unfortunately a consistent part of her life. I knew her story began when she was young, but I had no idea it had followed her into adulthood.

"This was my stepfather at the time, who, even probably still to this day has some kind of sexual fixation with me," Lola said, jumping headfirst into her story. As fun and happy as she is most of the time, she is also a no-nonsense businessperson when she needs to be. All signs of the eye-sparkling smile were absent as she became very serious telling me about her stepfather.

Lola said the fixation started at a young age, and because she was only 3 when it started, she feels the way she tells the story may be partially due to the way it was told to her "because I don't have a lot of actual vivid, detailed memories but do tend to have one consistent flashback, which is kind of crazy to me, but it's there."

She said, "It wasn't more that he did anything to me but what he had me do to him, so pretty much some touching and fondling in his bathroom, and that's what I can remember. I have the flashback of him sitting on that toilet and the red tile in that bathroom and just kind of a little bit of a visual of that, but I don't have any recollection of how I felt about it or what happened after that, like did I go run and say something? I don't know. From what I have built over the years and from what my dad has helped me piece together was that in one of the phone conversations when he called, I told him about this."

Lola lived with her mother, Beverly, and stepfather, Hunter, and her father called regularly to check on her. During one of the conversations, she revealed to him what had happened. She said he was "livid, appalled, blown away by it." He confronted Beverly about what Lola told him.

"Mom said, 'She's lying.' She pretty much buried it and was like, 'There's no way this ever happened.' My mom and stepdad had legal custody of me," Lola said. "He was kind of an influential person in the town we lived in and had money, so when it came down to legal stuff and custody, my mom ended up winning. My dad lived in Oklahoma, so there's that distance factor there. Hunter was a very physically abusive man to my mother. He's just that type of man that's sexually objective anyway, not that that's an excuse. For whatever reason, though, he has always fixated on me."

Besides the sexual fixation that she was aware of from such an early age, she was growing up watching Beverly and Hunter constantly fighting. Physical abuse was being normalized as a daily part of marriage.

"Did you ever actually see him physically abuse your mother or just see the aftermath?" I asked.

She replied, "Oh, absolutely. It was bad. It was very bad. I… mean…bad. Daily. They both drank. They would fight. She would go out. She was probably a little promiscuous and frivolous herself just because it was spiteful, and when she would come back, they would fight more. I'm talking like throwing things. There was one time I know she shot him in the leg. I know this sounds so crazy like a TV show, but they had a very physically abusive relationship, and I was so young, I don't know if I had anything to do with it. I have no idea. And I don't know that I've really let myself think that too much because that's not healthy."

And there it is.

Was this happening because of me?
Did I have some part in what was taking place?
Could I have done or said something to make this better?

Victim after victim asks themselves the same words in some form or another. Whether it's wondering about their assault, about how they dealt with it after it happened, about their role in negative relationships, about a gazillion and one things that had nothing to do with them like this, or about any number of other things, they question their role and whether they were somehow part of the cause of the chaos. Whether it's physical, mental, sexual, emotional, verbal, or fiscal abuse, the answer is nearly always the same; however, in their grief mindset, they rarely understand it.

"No. You were *not* the cause of this turmoil," I told her.

And, in Lola's case, if Hunter's sexual feelings for her *were* the root cause of their family's turmoil, it was still not Lola's fault. It was Hunter's fault for having those feelings for his stepdaughter – a child. It was also Beverly's fault for continuing to live with him and to fight with a predator because she was jealous of his feelings for her child rather than demand he leave to protect her daughter.

Understanding that is nearly impossible, though, when the memories you've lived with for so long are louder than rational thought.

Over time, being around Lola may have become too much for him to handle. When she was 6, Hunter suddenly announced Lola could no longer live with them and told Beverly she had to get out immediately. Lola still does not know exactly why he didn't want her there but wonders if he may have been having a difficult time controlling himself.

"I think that maybe it was just getting to be too much because he was like, 'She's got to go. Kick her out.' So, I ended up going to live with my dad in Oklahoma."

When she was 12, Beverly and Hunter finally filed for divorce. After years of denial, Beverly decided Hunter's sexual abuse of Lola was true and was a story that needed to be heard. Beverly called Lola's father to ask if Lola could come visit. Lola was happy to hear that her mother wanted to see her.

"Because she's never really been present and maybe because of some of the stuff that happened when I was young, for whatever reason, I used to put her on a pedestal," Lola said. "So, I was excited thinking, 'My mom wants me to come visit' and begging my dad, 'Can I please go visit my mom?' I had a stepmom with three daughters, so I had three stepsisters, and she and my dad have a younger son, so I was just the black sheep. I always have been. I'm just the outcast in the family. Dad and I connect, but I was thinking, 'Mom wants to see me!' Dad arranged it, and I came down to see her. I remember one day we were driving, and she said, 'We're going to court.' I said, 'Oh, okay. What are we going to court for?' I was 12. I didn't really know what we would go to court for. She said, 'Well, it's my divorce proceedings.'"

Lola said she was unsure what her part in the proceedings would be, but Beverly said she needed to be there, so she went along. When they arrived, they were greeted in a long hallway by a lawyer and Lola's maternal grandmother.

According to Lola, the lawyer said, "I'm so glad you were able to get Lola to be here to testify today."

"I was like, 'Wait, wait, wait! Testify about what?' They sat me down in this little room, and my mom and grandmother and this lawyer who I'd never met were telling me, 'We're going to put you on the stand, and you're going to testify about when Hunter molested you,'" Lola said, "I was like, 'Oh, no, no, I'm not. No, I'm not doing that. I'm sorry.' And they just said, 'Well, yeah, you are. You're a minor.' Mom still technically had legal custody of me. I said, 'No, we need to call my dad. Call my dad right now.' So, it was just a real forced manipulation, living back through it all over again. Mom said, 'And when you are up on the stand, you better say the right things.'"

Lola was 12, a child. She was ambushed and coerced into testifying about something that was a traumatic memory she had tried not to think of for so many years. To make matters worse, the icing on their manipulation cake was just getting started.

"I have a younger sister that my mom had with this man, and, for whatever reason, she has a very special place in my life. Like, that is my baby. I have a ton of siblings that are half or step, and she's a half sibling, but she is so special to me, and she is the only one I really say, '*That* is my sister,' and maybe it's because this man is her father," Lola said.

Knowing her relationship with her sister, Lola's mother used it against her. According to Lola, "They were saying things like, 'What if it happens to her?' And she was 6 at the time, and I was 12.

They basically said I had no choice. What was I supposed to do? So, I did it, and it was the most terrifying thing because I felt like I was lying because I didn't really know what I was talking about, and he was staring at me. His lawyer was brutal, and Mom was glaring at me like, 'You better not mess this up.' It was a lot of pressure, but I made it through. I just told what I had always been told versus kind of blended with what they said to say. I remember when I left there, my dad met us halfway. She had never told my dad any of it! I remember when I got in the truck, he asked what was wrong. I said, 'You are never going to believe what she made me do.' He was so angry. I was 12 then, and I didn't see my mom again until I was 16. He said, 'You are *never* going back.'"

Unfortunately, life with her father and stepmother was soon not much better than life with Beverly and Hunter. When her oldest stepsister became pregnant as a teenager, her parents became involved in a cult lifestyle that wouldn't allow certain holidays and actively preached against anything to do with sex or anything that resembled a penis.

"All that was awful and terrible and paganist," Lola said. "We couldn't go to churches with steeples on them anymore because steeples were phallic structures, and that's a perversion to the Lord. Sex has always been at the core of every negative thing in my life. It's hard to get past that."

The negativity with her father and stepmother ultimately led her to move back to live with Beverly when she was 16. Unfortunately, even though Beverly and Hunter were divorced, they were still in close contact.

"Mom and Hunter were divorced but still in this sick friendship where he bribes her with money," Lola said. "Basically, he's like, 'Well, if you shake your boobs in my face, I'll give you a loan for this.' I'm sure there's a lot more to it than that. He's just very objective. He feels like money is his power."

In her mother's case, Hunter is right. According to Lola, Beverly has always allowed Hunter's money to have power over her and continues to do so. When Lola moved back in with her mother at 16, Beverly wanted her to have a car. Hunter had a car available and said he could work out a deal for her to have it. One day while Lola and Beverly were at his home, the terms of the "deal" became apparent.

"We ended up over there sitting around talking, and come to find out part of the agreement is for me to take off my shirt with my mother in the room and basically stand in front of the door and lift my arms up and listen to comments about how beautiful my breasts are and how he wants to make a bronze bust of my bust and all these comments," Lola said, "and my mother is setting it up so now she won't have to pay any money for the car.

"And it was just kind of one of those experiences that I didn't know what to do because, again, it's my *mother*, and I've pretty much been gaslighted into, 'We have to have you a car. We've got to get you a car. We have to.' So, it was like, 'I guess this is what I have to do to get a car.' And this wasn't just two adults telling me this. It was two adults that have been in my life since *ever*. These were *parents*. My mom is still in my life."

Lola said she and Beverly never talk about that day. She said she knows "it sounds crazy" to say it isn't worth talking about, but, to her, it isn't. As she related the events of that afternoon, it was clear she still didn't want to discuss it after all this time, just as much as she didn't want to show off her breasts to her stepfather in front of her mother to get a car. She said she had no idea what would happen if she even tried to bring it up to her mother after all this time, so they never talk about it.

Over the years, Lola has been around Hunter on a regular basis, this man who assaulted her as a child and coerced her into stripping topless in front of both him and her mother while he made lewd comments for his own enjoyment in exchange for giving her a car when she was 16. She was forced to be around him in family situations pretending nothing had happened and expected to treat him like family for the sake of others who don't know what took place.

"So, over the years, up until just a couple of years ago, I have had to be in this man's presence, go to his home, stay there for a week of family gatherings," Lola said, "because for whatever reason, there's the money. 'Oh, well, just bring the family here for Christmas, and you can all stay at the cabin on the river,' he'll always say, so he creates that power. He did this when I was growing up after he and Mom divorced, and he continued to do it after I had a family of my own. I have been in situations where I had to owe him money, but it was for that control factor, because if he ever said to do something, and I told him, 'No,' he could say, 'Well, I loaned you that money….' I got to a point in my life, and it was just a few years ago, that I got out from under the financial situation. My mom paid him off for me. Then, I paid my mom off because I didn't want to have anything to do with him ever again. I'm done. I'm drawing the line. My mom said, 'I don't know why you're doing this.' I just told her it's my choice."

Lola now refuses to see Hunter. If Beverly is ever in the hospital, Lola said she "might" call Hunter if her mother "specifically requests it."

"The last time Mom was in the hospital, he called my phone for something minor, and I didn't answer," Lola said, "He can call someone else who knows what goes on. I know why he was calling me. He loves to get under my skin. He loves to torture me. It's a power play.

"He's still my little sister's dad," she said. "There's just such a weird dynamic there. I used to think I needed to be passive and cordial for my sister, but I decided I didn't have to do that anymore. When we would be up there for the summer to go to the river, I wouldn't take my shirt off, but he would still say things like, 'Sure do look good…' Well, my daughter looks just like me, and I can't even think about, 'What if he has thoughts like that about her?'"

Lola said, so far, Hunter has shown her daughter, Jolie, the type of attention he should show any other grandchild.

"There have been times," Lola said, "when Mom has had her that it makes me uncomfortable. The older she gets, the more she looks like me."

Lola's life took a turn away from Hunter's control when she met Jimmy.

"When Jimmy came into my life, I was like, 'I'm never getting married. I'm not having more kids. I'm a feminist. If you aren't good with that, then you can just carry your ass, 'cause I'm not doing this.' And he was like, 'Baby, I been fightin' the patriarchy for years, too!'"

Jimmy helped Lola look at life with a new perspective and look beyond the pains of the past.

"He has been really helpful. He told me, 'You have been abused continuously and you just deal with it because there is no other option, but you don't have to deal with it. You can say you aren't doing that anymore.' So, when it comes to Hunter now, I'm out."

It took a while for Jimmy's words and encouragement to normalize themselves into Lola's life, but she eventually distanced herself more from Hunter and his controlling behaviors. When her sister Sadie gave birth to her first child, Lola, Jimmy, and Jolie made the multi-state trip to visit. Sadie lives just up the road from Hunter, which made avoiding him difficult.

"We were supposed to go over there to have dinner one night, and Jimmy didn't want to go. I told my sister I didn't want to go over there either. By the grace of God, Sadie's gallbladder ruptured, and I couldn't help thinking, 'Man, way to take one for the team, Sis!'"

According to Lola, Sadie maintains a relationship with Hunter, even though he physically abused Sadie and caused her to have ongoing body image issues about her weight. Lola said Hunter never sexually abused her as far as she knows and has never done anything or said anything that indicated he objectifies her in that way.

He still saves those feelings, words, and gestures for Lola. Hunter has gone out of his way to develop a near obsession with her.

"He even tries to tell me he was at the hospital when I was born," she said. "He says he remembers seeing me when I was a baby and that he knew how special I was. I've asked my dad about that."

Her father said there is no way that story is true and that he does not know why Hunter would tell her that. Lola says she knows exactly why – because it gives him "one more way to get under my skin and fuels his obsession even further."

After all these years, after knowing what he did to her daughter at age 3, and after setting up what he did to her at age 16 in exchange for a car, Beverly still acts as if nothing is wrong. During the trip to meet Sadie's firstborn child, Lola, Jimmy, and Jolie were getting ready to go out when Beverly said, "Drive by and say 'Hi' to Hunter. His feelings are really hurt that he isn't going to see you."

Lola told Beverly in no uncertain terms that she could not care any less about Hunter's feelings if she tried.

"I said, 'I don't care about his feelings. If I go over there, I'm pushing him in the creek, and I hope he dies.' She said, 'Lola! Oh my God!' I said, 'You think I'm playing? I'm not going.' She was like, 'I don't know what's gotten into you.' I just don't know how to bridge that and don't know if it's even worth it. As we're on the way out the door, she was still saying, 'Think about it!'"

As they drove away, the route took them right by Hunter's home. As they drove past the driveway, Lola rolled down the window and said, "HEYYYYY!" When they arrived back at the house later that day, Beverly asked, "Did you drive by Hunter's house and say 'Hey?'"

"I told her, 'I did. I drove by, I rolled the window down, and I said, 'HEYYYYY!' She said, "Oh, my God, Lola!' and I said, 'I'm *not* going over there,'" Lola said, obviously very pleased with her reply.

Lola said she hasn't seen Hunter in several years and is happy to keep it that way.

"I don't want to, I don't need to, and I have no desire to," she said, "and my mom doesn't understand that. She's still in contact with him all the time because that's her lifeline for who knows what."

Putting Hunter and his control behind her was the fresh start Lola needed to place a spotlight solely on developing her family ties with Jimmy and Jolie and on making sure negative influences were barred from their world. Their little family flourished, and the more distance Lola put between her and Hunter, the stronger she became in her resolve to never allow him or anyone else to bring negative energy into their lives.

Raising Jolie in a world that sexualizes young women is a challenge, though.

"I am so freaking protective of Jolie, it's not even funny," Lola said, explaining that it's difficult to trust other people with her daughter when she knows that people she should have been able to trust did not protect her when she was younger.

A few months before our interview, Lola found out that Andrew (Jolie's father) and Brittany (Jolie's stepmother) had allowed one of Brittany's relatives to bring her teenage son into their home. While this would not be a problem under normal circumstances, according to Lola, this particular young man "was arrested for forcibly raping a 6-year-old boy on a school bus. He's a registered sex offender. I found out this boy had been let around my child, and nobody had given me any warning about this. When I found out about it, I did all my online research to the point my eye twitched for two days."

Lola was "so livid Jimmy picked me up from work so I didn't have to drive."

Lola said Jimmy told her, "I think what will make you feel better is if you go talk to Andrew about it."

Lola agreed but wanted to go immediately while the incident and her research were still spinning fiercely in her thoughts.

"I knocked on that door, and Andrew answered," she said. "I was visibly upset and said, 'I need to ask you a question, and if you are not honest with me, I swear to God…'"

Lola said she loves language and words and the use of them to make very clear, to-the-point arguments that leave nothing to the imagination. Andrew stared at her in blank surprise as she rattled off her questions rapid-fire like a prosecuting attorney prepared for battle.

"Is Todd a 17-year-old registered sex offender for forcibly raping a 6-year-old boy on a school bus?" she demanded. "Andrew said, 'Uhhhhh, I believe so.' I kept right on going and said, 'Well, I know so, because I have it pulled up right here! I've got a picture. I've got it all!' My knees were buckling. I probably looked like one of Sid's toys from 'Toy Story' spazzing out."

Lola said Andrew's first reaction was to claim it would be okay to have him around.

"Andrew said, 'Nothing's going to happen. I'll take care of it. I already told him if anything happens…'"

Lola's anger thinking back to that moment is apparent as if she were standing in the doorway once again, and I am not simply me sitting in front of her with a recorder, pen, and paper, but rather I am Andrew telling her once again that a 17-year-old rapist is perfectly acceptable to allow around her beautiful, innocent, developing "tween" daughter.

She continued with her recount of what she told him, almost looking right through me as if she were talking to him again that day as she said, "So your plan is to allow it to happen and then take care of it. No, no, no, no, no, no! So, I basically said, 'If I find out that this boy was around my daughter and you weren't there the entire time, I'm taking you to court, and I'm taking her away from you.' I've never threatened that. We do everything ourselves. We have no court involvement in our relationship. I said, 'I will take you to court, and I will take her from you.'"

Andrew said, "I hear you."

Lola said, "I'm telling you. You look me straight in the eye."

Later that evening, Lola returned when Andrew's wife, Brittany, was home. Lola said she once again made herself clear about how she felt about Todd.

"I said, 'I just want to make sure Andrew told you about our conversation we had today.' I was like full crazy. She said he told her, and I said, 'I want you to know how serious I am. I. Am. Serious.' She said, 'I get it,' and I replied, 'No, you don't get it. I can barely even look at you. You have a 10-year-old son. How do you let…' That's when she started with, 'Well, he's family, and….' I cut her right off and said, 'I don't care about what side of the family he's from.'"

Lola said that, unlike Andrew, Brittany had excuses about allowing Todd to come into their home.

"She said things like, 'Well, it's really hard, you know, when they just show up,' and I asked, 'You have no control over who crosses the threshold into your house?' I ended the conversation with, 'Here's what I said. I'm going to repeat it again.' I told her everything I had told Andrew that morning and everything I had already told her once," Lola said.

Lola said she felt eaten alive by the amount of guilt she was having about how much she had allowed Jolie to be around Hunter simply because he was "family." Having that conversation with Andrew and Brittany brought those feelings stinging to the surface and made her think of how many times she exposed Jolie to the man who had hurt her and her mother so many times throughout the years and continued to objectify and try to control her any chance he got.

"The flip side of it is that I had to sit down and talk to my child about it," Lola said. "I had to tell Jolie about Todd because she's got to know. So, of course, you could see the light dim a little because she didn't realize somebody she knew would do something like that. My daughter is not even a teenager, and I have already had to tell her what rape is, and 'here's a list of keywords to look out for.' The other day I asked Jimmy if we should buy her a rape whistle for when she rides her bike. I mean this is the world we live in. Well, at least it's the world I live in. It's what I think about all the time. Is she safe? Are men looking at her?"

After wearing a G-cup bra throughout high school and struggling with the size of her breasts into adulthood, Lola had a breast reduction in 2007. The attention and objectification from Hunter were merely a small part of wanting the reduction, though.

"I have had so much unwanted attention for having breasts. I don't want them," she said. "I wish somebody would take them away from me. Why do y'all act like that? I've literally had strange men be like, 'Ohhhh, my God…,' and I'm like, 'What the Hell is your problem?' to the point I wouldn't even get married. I told Andrew, 'I won't even marry you until I've had a breast reduction because all anybody ever says about me is my breasts, and it's so frustrating.' I struggled with intimacy a little bit with that. I actually am okay in a relationship that doesn't have a lot of sexual activity in it because there's too much pressure there. It's just too much. It's weird. But then, I think there's something wrong with me at the same time. There's a barrier that just doesn't let me."

Having those issues and barriers makes it even more difficult to raise a daughter in a world that sexualizes females at a young age. Lola and Jimmy are trying to teach Jolie to value herself while allowing her to be independent and make her own choices – a balance that is often difficult to achieve in strong-minded, creative adolescents.

"I'm teaching her to protect her body, to respect herself, and to understand that skin doesn't equal sexy," Lola said. "I understand sometimes we're going to wear things like a crop top, but that doesn't mean we're sexy. Jimmy says he wishes he could record me because I go off on these mom rants, and I end up with pretty good epiphanies at the end. One is basically, 'We don't give our cookies away for free.' Yes, I understand your body is changing and that you're more aware of things and you want to be 'sexy.' We all go through that. But we don't give our cookies away for free. You make people earn your cookies."

Lola said she is also trying to help Jolie understand that she is not required to be nice to someone just because that person expects it. She does not want Jolie to feel the pressure she felt from adults at such a young age to comply with requests she knew weren't right but that she felt she had to go along with to maintain family peace and make everyone happy.

She said she wants Jolie to understand, "You don't have to be nice to somebody just because they're there. You don't have to talk or smile at somebody just because they expect you to smile at them. You just don't have to. You're allowed to feel, but you don't have to make anybody feel like you have to give away something if you don't want to. She went through a phase of dressing like a hooker at home, and I was thinking, 'I don't know what's going on,' and then she started telling me that's how I dress, and I told her, 'Honey, you better back up. I do not dress like that. I do not dress like Sandy from *Grease*. Stop!' It made me worry that was how she was seeing me. I do dress sometimes, not provocative, but I like to look nice, you know? And she's over here thinking I look like a hooker. Of course, that's not what she's thinking, but when she's replicating it, I'm like, 'Child! That is not what I look like!'"

For Lola, education and transparency are the most important part of raising Jolie to understand how to protect herself.

"We educate her. I don't hold anything back," she said. "We caught her on YouTube searching, 'What does a penis look like?' We address these things head-on. I feel like information and knowledge are some of your best weapons against something happening to you because if you are more aware that it can happen, then you're more aware when it *is* happening. There's a lot of it you can't control unfortunately."

I asked Lola how she deals with people who cross the line in her everyday life coming from a past where there was abuse. For some survivors, small incidents can be hurtful and cause guilt and shame, but for others, they can cause anger. Still others move past them and brush them off as part of life.

"There is a man at work who's very touchy-feely," Lola said, rolling her eyes. "I say it's harmless. I know nothing would ever happen, but it's also not the most comfortable thing. We live in a world where tolerance is sometimes just what you have to deal with. You can't go on a crusade all the time everywhere. I wish we could.

I might lose my job. I can't stand old white men at all. It sucks that we live in a world where if you want to feel a little sexy it comes with a price. It comes with the territory. If you walk out of the house feeling like 'I like this. I like the way I feel. This looks good. Maybe my jeans are a little tight or maybe this is a little low-cut, but I feel good.' You still know you're probably going to have to deal with a little bit. You shouldn't have to."

I said, "I think there's a generation coming when that may not be as much of a thing."

Lola replied, "I don't think so either. I actually feel really bad for the boys who approach my daughter when she's a teenager. I'm not terribly worried. I tell her, 'I just want you to understand that as you're growing up, if you don't want to get married, you don't have to get married. If you don't want to have kids, you don't have to have kids.' And I also tell her, and this is just a little biased because I've been through three or four different types of relationships, but I say, 'Don't you love anybody unless they love you the way Jimmy loves me because it's just special.' This man still throughout the day is like, 'I love you! I can't wait to see you.' Things like that make a big difference. Don't find somebody who thinks it's their duty to have a wife. Find somebody who thinks it's a privilege to have a wife."

I asked Lola if Jolie knows anything about what had happened with Hunter or the way she had been raised by her father in Oklahoma to believe that all things related to sex were bad.

"Because I had to have this conversation with Jolie about Todd," she said, "she asked me if anything had happened to me. She doesn't know about the more recent stuff from age 16 on, but I did tell her I had an instance. She asked me how old, and I told her. She asked me who, and I told her. Again, I think knowledge and awareness are important. I also feel like because she knows and because she found out at a younger age, it's just something else that's going to make her more combative against it happening to her."

Lola is an example of the very definition of this book – she is more. She is not the girl Hunter took into the bathroom at 3 years old. She is not the teenager whose mother and former stepfather commanded her to stand topless in front of them while he made lustful comments about her in exchange for a car. She is not the daughter whose father and stepmother kneejerk-reacted to a teen-age pregnancy by forcing their children to shun the world around them and attempted to indoctrinate them to believe all things sexual were evil.

Lola is more.

"Despite all of that, it's just a list of things that happened," she said. "It's not who I am. If anything, it's fueled me to not let this be something that holds me back. I was so young, and then I was an adolescent. Now, as an adult, I'm very secure about who I am, but there's an awareness that it has shaped who I am. If I think about it, I get the flashback. I try not to think about it, I guess, but if I don't think about it, I'm not being vigilant of the world around me.

"I don't think what happened to me is nearly as bad as what has happened to other people, but there are so many different types of experiences that can go from absolutely terrifying to where you didn't even know something was happening. I just don't want people to be ashamed of things that happen to them. It's something that happened to you. It's like getting in a car accident or breaking your leg. It wasn't your fault. You can heal. You can move past it. It does not have to become something that weighs you down. It doesn't have to be something you're constantly ashamed of, and I think people should talk about it more. I think people should be able to come to a place where they can talk about it because not talking about it is what leads to its continuing to happen. So, any experience – if you were in a convenience store and someone came up and slapped you on the butt, that's harassment. That's abuse. You shouldn't have to stand for that. You should say, 'Hey! Don't slap me on my ass' as loud as you can for everybody to hear, but we don't, and we should."

Lola's stories deserve to be heard. She is an example of someone who took back her control from someone who was not only part of her assault but remained part of her life for years. Lola had to be more than just a moment and its aftermath. She had to be more than the accumulation of years of control, objectification, family abuse, and struggle to find her own voice in the midst of everyone who told her what to do.

Lola, you are more. So much more. You are rocking through this life as a mother, wife, sister, and friend to many, and you are far more dedicated as a daughter than anyone could expect you to be. You are more than what happened to you. You are more than what you probably thought about yourself at times. You are more than how your family failed you.

Lola said it best at the end of our interview when she said, "If all of us start telling our little stories, our medium-sized stories, our big stories – they're all our stories, and I think they all deserve to be heard."

They do. Every one of them. No matter how big or how small, including hers, and I am so thankful and honored she chose to share it here.

"Now, as an adult, I'm very secure about who I am,
but there's an awareness that it has shaped who I
am. If I think about it, I get the flashback. I try not to
think about it, I guess, but if I don't think about it, I'm
not being vigilant of the world around me."

Chapter Fifteen

Brandi

Sometimes, no matter how much therapy a person seeks or how many peace prayers they say day after day and night after night, scars of their sexual assault remain. They aren't scars that appear as nightmares that feel so real you can't tell they aren't or simple words someone says that trigger a breath-stealing, room-spinning anxiety attack.

Years later, a sexual assault victim may still deal with physical scars and pain just as much as lasting mental and emotional damage. More than a decade after her assault, Brandi wonders if she could have avoided some of the physical problems she continues to experience if she had been examined appropriately by a physician after her sexual assault.

"The next day when I woke up, I realized my body was covered in bruises," Brandi said. "I was injured by what he did and needed to see a doctor, but when I got the courage to tell my mom, she told me we had to lie to the doctor about what happened because I 'shouldn't have been such a slut and it wouldn't have happened.' I was probably never treated correctly due to not telling the truth of the extent of my injuries or how they occurred, but I'm not sure how to address it at this point."

Brandi's story is one of an acquaintance rape, a story all-too-familiar for many victims who trusted someone in a moment of weakness – in this case, a moment when alcohol was involved for a girl too young to handle its effects.

Brandi said her story was typical of a small-town Saturday night.

"I was 16 and went backroading with a few of my guy friends and a girlfriend I was supposed to be hanging with," she said. She told her mother she would be with only her female friend who was the same age, but, instead, she and the friend connected with a group of guys who were 5 to 10 years older.

As young people in small Southern towns often did at that time with little to no other entertainment options and no money to travel to towns where there was more to do, the group headed out into the country to ride around or do what they called "backroading," which often meant finding a place at a dirt crossroads or in a field to park and hang out.

"Around 10 minutes in, Brad, one of the guys, the 'cool' one all the girls wanted a shot with, offered me a drink," Brandi said. "I couldn't drink much because I would have to drive home later. I remember taking about two or three big drinks before I don't remember anything."

Brandi said she isn't sure how much time passed but guessed it was one to two hours.

"I woke up, and no one was in the truck but me," she said. "I tried to scoot toward the open door when I was pushed back down and heard, 'Where do you think you're going?' I didn't have the strength to get back up or move really and didn't know what was going on. I can remember my clothes being thrown on the ground outside the truck and, at some point, realized Brad was having sex with me."

At 16 years old, with her small build, and with the effects of alcohol still in her system, Brandi was no match for Brad, this man who was several years older and quite a bit larger.

"I don't remember really feeling any discomfort or anything else, other than confusion," she said. "When he was done, he helped put my clothes back on and told me someone took my car and we could go get it from them when I was okay to drive. Eventually I was able to drive – probably not safely – and on my way home."

When she was finally safe at home with the alcohol wearing off and her senses starting to return, the shock of what happened began to sink in. The sights, the sounds, the smells, the words, the feelings. All of it was becoming and feeling real with every passing moment as she sobered up and the numbness passed, both physically and mentally.

"I realized that something didn't feel right," Brandi said. Examining the physical damage Brad left behind on her body, she understood why she had the lingering feeling something more than sex had taken place. In her alcohol-induced numbness and desire to compartmentalize what was happening at that moment, she had been unaware that the assault included anal sex.

Brandi said, "I would never consider or consent to having sex anally, but apparently, I had or at least he thought I had."

Like many victims, Brandi has rationalized over the years that in her drunken state, she must have consented at some point to various parts of what happened, even though it is that very state that makes any sort of consent impossible. From what I've learned about her, though, I know her to be a rational person, someone who has experienced heartache in other areas of her life and made it through with a fearless face turned toward life's next phase with her signature smile to guide the way. Perhaps the belief that he somehow mistakenly thought she indicated willingness to participate is a coping mechanism, one that allows her to live in the same small town as Brad and deal with the ever-present physical scars as well as the mental and emotional triggers.

While it does not help her heal mentally or emotionally, Brandi does have the peace of mind in knowing she was not "such a slut," as her mother labeled her. In the years that have passed since that night, other girls and women have accused him of similar acts, and Brandi found out she was not the first person he sexually assaulted.

"I've definitely learned there are more victims, and he was even supposed to register as a sex offender when he was 18. He has been arrested for failure to register since then," she said, "but it still hasn't been enforced. I feel it would have saved a lot more girls, including me, from being his prey had he actually been on the registry where he belonged all these years."

Brandi has dealt with what happened to her as well as she could still living in the town where it took place surrounded by people who know this man and still having occasional opportunities to run into him while out with her husband and children. I asked how her husband felt knowing this had happened and whether he was fully aware of the details.

"He knows it happened," she said, "but I don't think I'd want to tell him everything in detail."

She is, of course, not the first survivor to tell me that. Whether it's a spouse, children, parents, or friends who are never told the story of what happened during a sexual assault, the people who want so badly to share what happened and give their voices a chance to be heard often live in silence. While they outwardly state that they aren't ashamed, they are also not prepared to discuss it with their loved ones, some out of fear of the reaction they'll receive and some simply out of a desire to not talk about it or to share the burden with loved ones.

"He took your choice away," I said. "You didn't have a choice to say 'No.'"

I wanted to reassure her that I understood she was a victim, that she had no choice in what took place that night, that she is a survivor.

While she might not have spoken up for herself when she was assaulted at 16 years old, the Brandi I have the honor of knowing is not the same person who was shoved down into the back of that truck years earlier or who wasn't able to seek appropriate medical care because of a mother who was too embarrassed to let anyone know what happened.

This Brandi has grown into an adult who makes herself known, has a mind of her own, and would not allow herself into the same situation a second time. My statement that she "didn't have a choice to say 'No'" must not have fallen on deaf ears at this stage in her life and healing.

"We all make plenty of mistakes, but being assaulted is not *our* mistake. It's theirs," Brandi said. "If it's even a mistake to them. You can be a high-end stripper giving a private dance while someone is throwing hundreds at you, but that doesn't mean you deserve to be touched without your permission. If you invite four of the five guys standing in the room to be with you, that doesn't mean number five gets a free pass. I've thought plenty of men were attractive, and yet I've never sexually assaulted any."

Brandi doesn't live her life in the fast lane giving private dances or seeking four out of five men, though. She has a quiet life with a loving, devoted husband who has had stars in his eyes for her since they were teenagers and sons she and her husband are raising to be Jesus-seeking, people-respecting men who someday will surely be as good of husbands as their father is to their mother. Role modeling the type of person they want their sons to be and showing them what love looks like in a relationship are important to Brandi and her husband, just as important as talking openly to them about sex.

"Either way it goes, boys or girls, there's just got to be 100% blunt transparency at some point," Brandi said of talking to young people about sex and relationships. "You can't sugarcoat it once they're old enough to know what sex is. Not that all predators are going to wait until a young person is 'old enough.' If I could lock my sons away or follow them everywhere, I probably would."

Brandi realizes locking her sons away is impossible and wouldn't be the healthy thing to do for them. Just as her parents once trusted her to go out into the world, she will someday have to trust that her children will make good choices and that the people with whom they associate will do the same. Unlike many young people, her sons will have the benefit of a mother who will talk to them openly, who will listen when they want to talk, and who will believe them when they say something isn't right.

Unfortunately, the feeling that something isn't right is a feeling their mother remembers, and it's a feeling that, hopefully, they will never experience. Their mother never healed 100% physically from her wounds, but she hopes her story will help others know they can heal mentally and emotionally.

"I'm sorry for anyone who has a story of their own to tell," Brandi said. "It takes a very weak person to rape someone. But you can be strong. It may not feel like it right now or even a year from now, but you can be. The person that did that to you is the weak one."

Brandi is such a strong example of what it means to be more than what happened during a sexual assault.

"I'd never let what Brad did to me define who I am now. We're all more than what he did to us, every one of us. All people who've been assaulted are more than their 'Brads.' When we decide we're more, we take back some of what they took from us."

CHAPTER SIXTEEN

Jessica

The first time Jessica learned about sexual assault, she was only 5. At that age, she barely knew boys and girls were different for reasons other than girls having long hair and wearing dresses while boys cut their hair short and wore pants or girls wanting to have tea parties while boys played with toy trucks. Her world was stereotypical and safe, and her understanding of it was limited to what a textbook, normal 5-year-old should know.

The summer before she started kindergarten, she was playing one afternoon at the home of a church friend, as children often do. Her friend's older brother, who was in his early teens, was there as well.

"I had to go to the bathroom," Jessica said, "and the door opened. It was the brother. He locked the door behind him, bent down in front of me, and told me to open my legs. I didn't really know what else to say, so I was like, 'Okay…' because, to me, he was an adult, and I'd been taught to do what adults told me to do."

Looking back at the incident now, Jessica realizes there should have been red flags when he told her to "open her legs," but she was 5 years old. In her innocence, the trouble she might get into by not doing what an adult told her to do far outweighed any need to question what he was demanding. She had never been exposed to anything sexual or had to worry about the people in her life and had every reason to trust that this young man had her best interest at heart based on what she knew of the world in her small, sheltered corner of it.

"And, so, there he was on his knees in front of me with his hands between my legs touching a place I had been told was private, and he said, 'Yeah, it looks just like my sister's.' I just looked at him and said, 'Oh. Okay.' I didn't know what else to say. I remember being so scared."

Jessica said he insisted that she not tell her parents what happened because, "you'll get in trouble for this."

She did tell her friend about it, though, and her friend's reply was one of indifference, which made Jessica wonder if she overreacted.

Her friend simply shrugged and said, "Yeah, he does that to me all the time."

It wasn't until years later that Jessica finally told her mother.

"It was like I blocked it out for so long," she said. "Then, we drove by their house one day, and Mom happened to say, 'Hey, do you remember those people?' I told her what happened with my friend's brother, and to say she was mad doesn't begin to describe how she reacted. She was screaming, 'I'll kill him!' Of course, it was too late. So much time had passed, and it would just be my word against his. I'm sure he would claim I was making it up for attention or not remembering exactly what happened since I was so young at the time. You don't forget things like that, though."

From the look on her face and the way she let the last words trail off, there was no question she remembered every detail of that afternoon. So often, people question the validity of a child's memories as flawed because children – especially younger ones – sometimes embellish their memories and put a different spin on reality. However, memories like these tend to stand out with exceptional clarity for people who relive them many times in their minds over the years.

Jessica said she prayed for the sister and for the brother, too, over the years. She wondered sometimes after she told her mother and began thinking of the incident if they maintained their sibling relationship after they became adults. She also wondered if someone had abused the brother, which prompted him to abuse others. She said she tried not to hold onto negative feelings toward him, but it was a scary incident to go through at such a young age, and it made her question who could be trusted in her world.

When she was a teenager, she was victimized again, but this time, her questions of trust went deeper and were hurtful on a more personal level. She was not only assaulted on the high school bus but was unable to get the help she so desperately needed, both during and after the incident.

"I rode the bus pretty often, and I was friends with a lot of guys because as a young girl, sometimes you're like, 'Oh, it's less drama being friends with guys,' and also what girl doesn't like a little bit of attention from young football players? I know it sounds terrible to say, but it's just true," she said, laughing. One thing I learned about Jessica as we talked is that she is a transparent straight shooter who won't sugarcoat, not even if it means calling herself out.

"I was sitting on the bus, and this day was assigned seating because we were on the bus for a specific purpose. I was sitting with this boy named Trey, and we were just joking around and talking, and the next thing I knew, he had one hand up my shirt and his other hand down my pants. I said, 'Whoa! What are you doing?' My best guy friend Scott was sitting in front of me, and I said, 'Can you help me out back here?!' So, Trey was all of a sudden on top of me, and Scott just looked back, and I practically shrieked, 'Help me!'"

As Jessica tried to push Trey off of her and begged Scott to intervene, the only adult on the bus was the driver who couldn't hear what was going on. She said she finally managed to push Trey off of her, even though she was about half his size. Other students sitting in the area turned a blind eye to what was going on as she struggled, making the situation even more frustrating.

"I hit him as hard as I could," she said, "and he called me a bitch and a slut. I went to our principal to report it as soon as I got the chance. I was bawling because, oddly enough, I thought I was going to be the one who got in trouble for it. It sounds so crazy now, but at that age and as upset as I was, it totally made sense to me at the time."

The principal told her it would be addressed, but when she got called back to the office for a follow-up meeting two hours later, she was not greeted with the understanding help she had anticipated.

"The principal said, 'Well, Trey says you were asking him to do these things,' and I couldn't believe what I was hearing. I turned to the principal and hollered, 'No! Then why would I come to you with it? Why would I do that?' I was even more surprised when he said, 'Not only that, but Scott is backing up his story saying it was all you.' I was like, "No, no, *no*! Not only did I endure something traumatic, to say the least, but I can't even safely tell anyone about it because then it's my fault.'"

She was still clearly upset after all these years.

"They definitely had each other's backs on that," she said. "That was so disappointing to me because how can you call yourself somebody's friend and then see something that they don't want being done to them and you don't even step forward to help them or at least try? And even if the principal thought I wanted him to do those things, why did he act like this was acceptable bus behavior? My head was spinning like crazy when I left his office. I felt like I was the one who had done something wrong and they were laughing at the silly, crying girl who got upset over something she was asking for."

I asked how she feels knowing this is the world in which her daughters are growing up.

"Unless my daughters give me a reason to question their story, I will always believe them if they confide in me that something has happened," Jessica said. "Definitely, and I hope to God that they don't feel too scared to come to me with it because I was definitely too scared to go to my parents. I didn't feel like I could talk to my parents about anything at all or at least I didn't think I could."

Jessica said she is comfortable talking about most things, even if a topic comes up that isn't easily discussed. She hopes her children will find a way to openly talk through whatever issues or questions they have because she doesn't want them to ever feel as she did that afternoon when she left the principal's office feeling "dismissed and worthless."

"I don't know that it would be difficult talking about something like that. What I do know is that I want them to always know they don't have to feel ashamed," she said. "Even if they had sex with someone before, if it's not consensual, it's not consensual, and if I have to share these stories to make them feel comfortable that they can come to me, absolutely I will. I would be comfortable telling them anything."

Unfortunately, that was not the relationship she had with her parents growing up. She explained that she and her father had a complex relationship complicated by divorce. Things shared between them tended to become blown out of proportion with blame regularly misplaced.

"My home didn't feel like a safe place, even though no abuse ever took place there," she said.

Managing one-on-one relationships can be difficult for people with tenuous family connections who are also carrying burdens related to assault. Jessica navigated through her teen years dealing with these issues and found herself in a serious relationship at 16 years old. During the year she and her boyfriend were together, a series of traumatic events took place that bonded them on an unusually close level for a couple their age. His younger sister died in an automobile accident not long after he and Jessica began dating, and going through the funeral and mourning process by his side made Jessica feel bonded to him and to his family.

When he moved to a town about an hour away, they stayed in touch and considered themselves to be dating long-distance. When he came into town one weekend, Jessica went to his grandfather's house to visit.

"This is the boy I lost my virginity to, so it wasn't like sex was off the table, but that day, for me, it was because I had started my period," she said. "I went to his grandfather's house, but as soon as I got there, he was excited and met me at the car as soon as I drove into the driveway. We were there alone, so he grabbed my hand, walked me through the house to the back room, and didn't even really talk to me. He pushed me down on the bed, and I said, 'No, I don't want to today,' and all he said was, 'Did I ask you if you wanted to today?' I sort of laughed and said, 'Ha. Ha. Funny.' I thought he was joking."

Without giving her time to realize what was happening, he pulled her pants off and "was in me, and I yelled, '*Please! Stop!*' and he just said, 'It'll just take a minute,'" Jessica said. And it did, according to her. In barely more than a minute, he was finished while she lay on the bed stunned, worried that no protection had been used and overwhelmed by what had taken place.

As soon as it was over, she pulled up her pants and quickly left.

"I was mad," she said. "I left, and I cried the entire way home. What do you do when something like that happens and you're just in complete shock and you can't believe someone you trusted would treat you like that? I thought I loved him. I thought he loved me, but then he treated me that way."

She paused, closed her eyes, and sat in silence for a few seconds before continuing. When she opened her eyes, I could tell she was very centered on what she was about to say.

"You think, as a young girl, that you'll be such a badass if something like that happens to you. You're like, 'Oh, I'll beat him up. I'll come up fighting like a warrior. I wish he would try to lay a hand on me!' But then it happens to you, and you're just left in this mess crying your eyes out. I was terrified. I've never really told anyone it wasn't consensual. That guy really did a number on me."

From the pain in her eyes, anyone can see he certainly did and continues to, deep down in a place she doesn't like to go. It's a place reserved for teaching her daughters how to defend themselves. It's also a place she draws from daily as she teaches her youngest – her son – how to treat women with respect and dignity and how to understand that people have a choice at all times in all things, especially where their bodies are concerned.

Jessica said the incidents she went through affected her ability to trust both men and women, but she doesn't believe that is uncommon among assault survivors.

She said, "I don't know why people are afraid to speak up; however, in more recent years, I feel like women have come so far in standing up to social injustices like that. Definitely I've had trust issues, intimacy issues – you name it – psychological stuff. I've dealt with anxiety most of my life, and when things like that happen, it certainly doesn't help."

Thinking back to her assaults is something she does a lot more now that her daughter Amelia is getting older because, according to Jessica, she constantly worries. She thinks about the little girl she was at her friend's house who was too unfamiliar about was happening to know she could tell the older brother "No" and wonders if she has educated and empowered her daughter enough to know better without also going through the world afraid. She thinks about the teenager she was on the bus whose trust was broken when a classmate assaulted her and one of her best friends not only failed to come to her aid but refuted her story when she needed his support. She thinks about the boyfriend who forcefully took what he wanted from her as if she were his possession despite her refusal and pleas for him to stop.

Jessica said she was in a bad place where men were concerned for a long time. Throughout their marriage, her ex-husband knew what happened with her boyfriend because it stuck out to her as a moment in a relationship when she tried to say "No" and was betrayed by someone for whom she cared deeply. When they first married, she shared the assault with him as a defining moment that shaped her as a person, her ability to trust, and her approach to relationships.

However, during our interview she told me there were quite a few other times she didn't want to engage in sexual activities but her boyfriend pressured her into it or simply took his liberties as he could find opportunities to do so. She had never spoken about most of the incidents, even with her ex-husband. While the assault at the grandfather's house wasn't the only time he took advantage of her, it was the only time his actions escalated with such sudden force. The other times occurred mostly with coerced consent after her resistance had been worn down. Because of that, Jessica never told anyone. Like many women, she felt that because she gave in, no one would believe that she didn't "want it."

"There was a time we were going to church camp, and I was riding in the back of my youth leader's truck," she told me. "My boyfriend stuck his hand down my pants when I didn't want him to. It's little random things like that which boys think they can get away with. You know I've talked to the woman that was driving the truck since then, and she said she knew something was going on. She said she wished I would have said something. I wish I had said something, too. Sure would've saved me some issues."

Jessica said she thought meeting and marrying her husband would "save her." The man she dated before she met her husband, Sean, was "so mean and controlling. The last straw for me was when he announced he was going to be a mixed martial arts fighter and was showing me a move. He decided without telling me that he was going to try it out on me. When he kicked me, I was on the floor. He kept kicking me, and he was standing over me laughing about it. I was lying on the floor crying and thinking, 'Okay, new plan – get all of my things and get out of here!' I was so messed up in the head and misfiring that I really thought I was supposed to keep a positive attitude and wait for things to get better. I kept telling myself, 'I have to get through this hard part first.'"

Jessica said she knew that wasn't the path she wanted for her life, but, like many women, she had thought she could make the best of it since she was already in the situation. Having always been close to her older brother, she finally let go and moved on when he told her, "You don't have to live this way. You don't deserve this. You could have and you need so much better."

"Hearing my brother say that changed everything. I think I knew those things somewhere in my mind, or at least I wanted to believe they were true, but just to hear somebody that you respect so much say something like that to you is important. It really changed my course, changed my path," she said. "People don't understand why women can't just walk away from a bad situation or see why the life they're living isn't where they need to be or what they deserve, but when you've been living it for long enough, it's hard to see the reality of what could be. All you see is what is. Sometimes having someone you love come along and remind you to open your eyes is all it takes."

Meeting her husband changed her path at that time in her life. He was a youth pastor at a local church, had a stable job, and, on the surface, treated her differently than other men. He was kind, patient, friendly, and, at first, didn't try to put his hands on her all the time. She was convinced if she told Sean the types of things she had been through or the types of things she had done, he wouldn't want anything to do with her. In fact, when they began talking, she was secretly having sex with one of their coworkers.

"I was keeping Sean at arms' length and telling him very clearly, 'I. Don't. Want. To. Date. You.' His response never varied. Every time, he smiled the nicest smile and looked right at me and said, 'But you're going to.' One day he asked, 'Why? Why don't I want to date you?' so I just came right out and told him that if he knew who I was, he wouldn't want to date me."

Sean asked Jessica to tell him a single thing that would shock him.

"I'm sleeping with Marcus," she said, very matter-of-factly revealing that she, at age 20, was having sex with their 18-year-old coworker.

"Gross. Okay," he said. "So, stop."

Jessica replied, "Okay, I will. You know I also drink and smoke pot."

Sean was unmoved.

"Okay, cool. Cool story. You know you don't have to do that to have fun," he told her.

Jessica didn't quite know how to reply to the youth pastor sitting across from her, so she simply pointed at herself and sarcastically said, "Well, you know, this is not what you want to bring to church to meet your preacher. This is not somebody you want to introduce to Mama."

Sean – and his mother and his pastor – disagreed. Several years and four children later, Jessica and Sean were still married and seemingly, mostly happy. They owned their first home, worked through problems, and loved each other despite whatever broken paths they traveled before meeting. They attended church faithfully every week, and, perhaps much to the surprise of the young girl still inside Jessica, no one turned her away as Sean proudly walked her in to greet the congregation and pastor every week.

Reaching that point in their marriage had been a rocky road, though. The outwardly kindhearted, patient, youth pastor did not initially have a compassionate approach to their marriage's intimate side. According to Jessica, Sean's attitude toward sex was, "'We're married now. The Bible says you belong to me.' He felt like he could put his hands on me whenever he wanted and that I needed to be okay with it. I understand the whole thing about being young and in love and newly married, but at some point, I needed a break, especially coming from where I'd been with a boyfriend who thought he owned me and knowing Sean understood how that made me feel. Or at least I thought he did."

Jessica said she tried not to push him away, but his sexual determination was relentless.

"He was obsessed," she said. "If we were together in the house, he had to have his hands on me. It was like he had this idea that he hadn't been with that many girls before me, and he'd led this nice, good-guy life, so now that he was married, it was supposed to be all sex all the time. He tried to hold the Bible over my head every chance he got, but I knew better."

Jessica said she knew his interpretation of 1 Corinthians 7:4 wasn't correct, but he didn't appreciate having it pointed out to him.

"He thought he knew more than I did," she said. "He always treats me like he automatically knows more than I do just because he's a man. He certainly got his ears full, and he didn't like it one bit. He needed to understand that I could just as easily tell him, 'Oh yeah? Well, I own you now, too, and I'm shutting you down for the night!'"

She laughed as she told me how she explained that the full verse states, "The wife does not have authority over her own body but yields it to her husband. In the same way, the husband does not have authority over his own body but yields it to his wife."

"He was more than happy to tell me the first part every time he got a chance and try to hold me to it without acknowledging that last part," Jessica said. "When I reminded him that the verse actually refers to how we're married and ownership is shared, he wasn't happy, to say the least."

When she told him she would no longer allow him to hold a "we're married now" directive over her head or have his hands all over her whenever he wanted (especially not in front of their daughter who was finally old enough to notice what was going on), he pitched a fit like a toddler in timeout – not behavior befitting a grown man and certainly not the behavior of a loving husband trying to be romantic with his wife.

Throughout their marriage, Sean complained that their sex life did not keep up with his demands.

"He kept telling me we weren't having enough sex, but we were together at least twice a week pretty much the whole time we were married," she said. "From what other people have told me and what

I've read, I'd say that's a fairly decent sex life for married people, and it seemed to me he was more than satisfied. If he wasn't, he did a great job of pretending. I thought we were both in a happy place in our life, but I guess something was missing for him."

With Sean often out of town for work a week or more at a time and in odd moods when he was in town, Jessica often wondered if he might be looking to other women to meet his insatiable sexual needs. The topic came up a few times early in their marriage, but he persistently denied it. Jessica tried to believe him. Their life was happy overall, and she chose to believe the man she built a life, a family, and a home with was so in love with her that he couldn't possibly get enough of their time together. With four children and the stress of daily life, she convinced herself it was normal to crave one-on-one time to a higher degree sometimes.

Jessica said, "Honestly, I wanted to believe he was just such an amazing, devoted husband who adored me so much that after seven years of marriage and four kids and being through so much together, he genuinely wanted me more than ever, so when he complained about our sex life, I tried to remind myself that even though I might be tired or not feel like doing anything, I needed to get in there and take one for the team, so to speak. I really thought our sex life was great, but he never seemed to think it was enough."

When Sean announced he wanted a divorce shortly after their seventh anniversary, he complained she had pushed him away, that she wasn't affectionate enough, and that she wasn't available when he wanted her. Jessica was pursuing her bachelor's degree full-time, and there were four children in the house she was often left to raise on her own while he was out of town, which she somehow successfully managed even with diagnosed anxiety problems. Knowing her history of anxiety and knowing that she was often left alone with the children and might need help, she voiced her concerns about the remote location he chose when they bought their first home. However, he was adamant, and she ultimately agreed when she saw how happy he was.

"I never wanted that house," she said, "but he wouldn't talk about anywhere else once he saw it. I felt like we were so far from anyone we knew. He liked that. I hated it. He was out of town so much, and I was stuck out there with the kids all by myself. It was a very isolating feeling. He got to get out and see things and go out of town for work, and I was stuck at home. The only places I ever got to go were to church, to the school, and the store, for the most part. I had a few classes I had to go to, but most of my classes were online. With such a big family, we didn't even really go out to eat. Looking back, I wonder if he was isolating me to keep me out of his business, but I don't know. I may be reading too much into it."

Jessica will probably always have more questions than answers. Prepared to fight for their marriage, she asked Sean to go to counseling as soon as he asked for a divorce, but he didn't want to spend the money on a sitter and a counselor. She tried to give him as much attention as he could possibly want and shower him with sex and love, purchasing seductive lingerie and whatever else might interest him. She told him she thought they had a good relationship but that if his needs weren't being met, she would step up her efforts to make him feel loved and wanted.

His response was, "All I see in your eyes is fear right now."

"He thought I was doing all those things to save the roof over my head and a few dollar signs in the bank account," she said. "I'll admit that there was a time early in our marriage when I was in a different place in my life when I might have thought, 'Sean will make a good first husband.' By this point, though, I had grown up. I wasn't the screwed-up kid sleeping with a coworker who needed the youth pastor to save me from myself. I was a grown woman with a husband I loved and four kids and a life we'd created together that I thought he wanted to be part of, too. I wasn't afraid to lose a roof and some money. I was afraid to lose the man who stood by my side holding all of it together."

Jessica slammed the table with her hand in frustration and shoved her chair back almost knocking it over. She paced the room for a few minutes taking time to gather her thoughts, to breathe, and to calm down, as others have also done when telling me their stories and reaching a peak emotional moment. Normally, she speaks in fairly low, composed tones with a quietness in her voice that's often punctuated with small laughs that snuggle around the edges of her words and further animate her expressive eyes. For her to lash out with such an outburst of enraged resentment and pull back a hand that was red for several minutes as she continued talking is foreign to the person I know her to be. That abrupt type of reaction is not foreign, though, in these stories filled with so much raw emotion.

Settling back into her chair, she looked me directly in the eye as she said with great purpose and anger still plainly right below the surface, "Throughout our entire marriage, this man made me feel like I had to prove to him that I loved him, like I had to work every day to prove to him I wasn't cheating, like I had to always prove I wasn't the girl he somehow saved back when we were working together. He practically bullied his way into my life, and suddenly after seven years of marriage he announces he wants a divorce, and I'm somehow supposed to feel like it was all my fault because he was so mistreated all those years. He wasn't mistreated. He was sleeping with one of his coworkers, a girl I specifically asked him about I can't count how many times, and he denied it every single time. He certainly couldn't deny it after he got caught on camera sleeping with her in the office."

Sean admitted to an ongoing sexual relationship with his coworker. Not long after they separated, Jessica and Sean met one night to discuss their marriage and the details of what happened. Jessica recorded the conversation and played it for me during our interview. Throughout the recording, Sean remained narcissistically calm as he stated he was pushed into the affair by Jessica's failure to meet his sexual needs during their marriage and by her own cheating.

"I never cheated on him, and he knows that," Jessica said. "He took conversations with an old friend far out of context and put words in my mouth. I never did anything other than speak to someone he didn't like from when I was younger. I never crossed a line other than the imaginary lines he created for me. If it's inappropriate to ever speak to another man once you're married without suspicion that you're cheating, then I guess there are a whole lot of women in trouble. If I had anything to hide, I wouldn't have told him about it. He should know that since he hid *his* relationship for so long. You can't hide from those cameras, though. He and his girlfriend both got fired, and he still had no remorse."

Unfortunately for her family, three of their children were in the home as long-term foster placements. One was an older teenager who was able to stay long enough to move out on her own when she turned 18 not long after Jessica and Sean separated. Because of their guidance, she moved on with her life in positive ways and has been on a much better path than she would have been without them. She has a stable job and still attends the church to which they introduced her where she began her faith journey and was baptized while she lived with them.

The other two foster children, however, were a younger sibling pair Jessica and Sean were preparing to adopt. They called them "Mama" and "Daddy." Their biological daughter Amelia proudly claimed them as her younger sister and brother, and Jessica and Sean's mothers had naturally and happily stepped into their roles as grandmothers, showering the children with attention and love, two things they had not previously known in their brief, unstable lives.

Sean's refusal to seek counseling and, ultimately, his affair, not only ended their marriage but also split up siblings who faced an uncertain future after leaving the safety of what had become their family.

"Losing my kids breaks my heart more than losing Sean most days," Jessica said. "That's terrible. I know. If it makes me a terrible person, so be it. I worry about them every day, and I pray for their safety. They came from such a broken home. Being with us was a chance for a new life. I wanted to adopt them on my own, but when we divorced, I had nothing. I'm hopeful I'll be able to stay in touch with them and continue to be a small part of their lives."

Sean managed the family's financial affairs and agreed he would continue doing so after he and Jessica separated. After he lost his job, he picked up odd jobs for a while to make ends meet without seeking full-time employment. He left Jessica with no money for basic necessities. Living in a community property state, Jessica attempted to withdraw half of the money they had in a joint checking account so she could at least buy food. Sean demanded she return it so he could pay bills, including the mortgage on the isolated house Jessica continued to live in due to lack of financial options to move elsewhere. Reluctantly, Jessica redeposited the money but regretted the decision.

"That was before I knew for sure he had been sleeping with that other woman," she said. "At that point, I was still holding out hope that he would agree to counseling and the whole episode of our lives would somehow be a distant memory sooner than later. I put the money back and told myself I was overreacting. It sure didn't feel like an overreaction when I was looking around at a pantry and a refrigerator that were quickly emptying out."

Her older brother who had been the voice of reason in her life so many years before stepped in yet again to help his little sister in a time of need and sent money for a month's worth of groceries. Jessica's mother helped her secure a job in her hometown in another state so she and Amelia could move from the isolated home they had shared with Sean and relocate closer to family and a stable support system.

Jessica was steadily praying about how to handle the family situation with her foster children. As much as she wanted to adopt them, she knew she had to make a life for Amelia and for herself, and the small amount of income she was going to get at the new job would barely be enough for them to establish themselves and get by. It would certainly not be enough to cover the costs of raising three children and completing the adoption process.

"I was broken," Jessica said. "I walked in the girls' room and watched them sleeping so quietly. Amelia had crawled into bed with her little sister, and they were so sweet. Breaking them up was one of the hardest things I've ever had to do, and I don't think I'll ever forgive Sean for tearing our family apart. I pray every night to find forgiveness, but I'm still working on it."

For Jessica, that has been the most difficult part of her divorce – forgiving her husband for making her feel sexually bullied throughout their marriage and for eventually allowing his sexual obsession to tear their family apart.

"Sometimes, I look around and think, 'Why is this world so controlled by sex?' Seriously. It's everywhere – commercials, movies, music, books, casual conversation. Young kids learn about it far too soon, and, so often, just like with me and my friend's brother, it's not in a way we'd really like for them to learn, you know? Men think they can paw at their wives any time they want to and hang that Bible verse over their heads about owning us. Women walk around like every man is going to rape them, when we all know – or at least I hope we do – that there are plenty of really great guys out there.

"If I can still believe that, I know there are other women who can, right? I mean, give me a break. After all the things I've been through and a husband who was a jerk about sex for seven years and then tried to blame me for making him have an affair, if I can still believe there are good men who aren't out to get me, surely there are others who agree with me that not all men are out to hurt women."

I assured Jessica she was not alone and that one common thread throughout the interview process for this book was that most women who had been assaulted still knew deep down that not all men were out to get them. Even though they had increased their levels of caution and improved their approaches to safety, they still wanted love and relationships and passion. For the most part, they did not reject sexual relationships, and they realized not all people in their lives were going to hurt them.

"What are you doing to heal from this?" I asked, mostly interested to see if her answer would mention anything about how she was healing or if it would once again center on what she was doing to make a life for Amelia and ensure that her other children were safe.

"I'm praying," Jessica replied. "I'm breathing. I'm trying not to be mad. Then, sometimes I get mad, and I'm okay with it, but I don't let Amelia see that. She doesn't need to be part of that anger. There will come a time when she has questions, and I'll answer them as best I can, but I think those questions are for her father to answer how he sees fit. She's a smart girl, and she'll see through most of his answers, I'm sure. I also try to make mental lists of all the things in our life that we have to be thankful for. I try to remind myself that not all men are like Sean.

"Then, I remember how I felt when I met him and how I felt like he was saving me in a way. I remind myself I don't want to feel like that again. Then, I feel strong. I feel like I'm at the beginning of something, like Amelia and I are setting out on a path that's going to be something great and maybe, just maybe, I'm going to not only be okay but better than ever. For the first time in my whole life, I'm on my own and nobody is telling me what to do or how to do it or why it's not good enough."

Hearing the right words at the right time when she was younger – in that case, from her older brother – and letting down her walls to allow the seemingly right person in with whom she could share her heart made all the difference for a woman who experienced potentially lifelong emotional damage at the hands of multiple assaulters. Several years later, though, as life seemed to be crumbling around her, Jessica realized that the person who actually helped her was the only person who can truly help any of us. Jessica helped herself back then, and she was the only person who could truly help when she went through her divorce because of her willingness to dare to imagine a different life and to be ready to let go of the pain of the past.

And because Jessica forged a new, brighter, happier path for herself, she will be better able to guide her daughter down a better path as well. Perhaps Amelia – and maybe even Jessica's foster children who were guided by her love and influence while they were in her care – can be spared the pain Jessica experienced because of the courage she found to move on.

"People don't understand why women can't just walk away from a bad situation or see why the life they're living isn't where they need to be or what they deserve, but when you've been living it for long enough, it's hard to see the reality of what could be. All you see is what is."

Chapter Seventeen

Karen

Forty years later, Karen spoke candidly as she recounted her sexual assault. Before we sat down to talk, I'd never had the honor of meeting her outside brief text exchanges and a private online group created by mutual acquaintances. Hers was the first survivor story I had no prior knowledge of before we met to talk, so I approached the interview with nervous anticipation as I waited for the video chat box to pop up on the screen.

On the other side of a slightly grainy video connection from several states away, a fresh-faced 50-year-old woman appeared on my laptop. While the video connection may not have been the sitting-right-beside-me effect for which I had hoped, the determination in Karen's voice was unmistakable as she spoke. After hardly a moment's pleasantries, her words came across the microphone with unswerving resolution.

This was the day her story would be told, and Karen was ready to be heard.

"I was 10 years old," she said. "I've been trying to go back and figure out how many places we had lived by the time I was 10 but at least 10 places, maybe more. My mom had a new boyfriend, so it came to the point where he had to talk to us about discipline. He told me he would talk to me separately because I was older."

Karen has two younger sisters, and her mother's boyfriend Paul has two younger sons who lived with them. His two younger daughters rarely visited. Karen was the oldest of all seven children.

"He said it made no sense to talk to me the same as them because they were younger," she said. "That made sense to me."

At 10 years old, children tend to accept the word of an adult in authority, at least to some degree, even if they aren't happy about it, especially when that adult is talking about discipline and the child perceives she might get in trouble. Karen felt that if Paul wanted to talk to her about discipline separately from the younger children, she must have different rules since more would be expected from her.

Karen and her sisters had met many men in their short lives who were introduced as their mother's boyfriends, but they hoped their mother would keep Paul around for a while because he owned a ranch with a large amount of land.

"He had horses and tons of land and beautiful raspberry bushes that I got to go and pick, and everything was great," Karen said. "I listened to him talk to my sisters and his kids. He told them that they would get spanked or beat if they didn't listen."

For Karen, Paul had a different plan. She said when it came time to talk to her about how he planned to discipline her, he took her into his bedroom.

"He told me that I would never get disciplined if I would do what he wanted, and I asked what that was."

He said, "Have you ever heard of a penis?"

Karen replied, "No."

He said, "Have you ever heard of a vagina," and, again, she said, "No."

Karen said Paul couldn't believe she hadn't heard of either of those things.

"He said, 'You haven't had sexual education yet? You're 10 years old,' and I said, 'I know a little bit about it.' Then he said, 'Do you want to feel one?' and I said, 'No.'"

Karen said at that moment, she felt something was "not right," but as a child who was facing an adult with the power to put her family out on the street if she angered him and who had just heard other children be told they would be beaten if they didn't obey, she was frozen with uncertainty.

So far, he had mentioned nothing about discipline. Karen knew she was uncomfortable with the things Paul was talking about but unsure what private body parts and sexual education had to do with how he planned to discipline her.

Karen said that was when her feeling that something wasn't right began to make sense. At that point, the "discipline discussion" turned into sexual assault.

Karen closed her eyes between sentences, took short but deep breaths, and turned her head slightly to the side away from the web camera as she repeated the words he said to her. The frightening moments hung heavily in the air one by one for a brief moment as she tried to move quickly through them.

Even though so many years have passed, and she has fought her way from broken child to rebuilt woman who put the past's pains behind her, the 10-year-old little girl's anxiety and disorientation were right beneath the surface in the strained voice coming across the computer – less because of a crackling video link and more because of a cracking voice connected to a still-damaged heart.

Paul's next question made it clear what was on his mind when he asked, "Could I touch you between your legs?"

Karen replied, "No."

He pushed her further asking, "Well, haven't you ever thought about feeling good down there?"

Again, Karen said she replied, "No."

As she tried to tell me her story, she paused again. I told her to take as much time as she needed. Forty years of pain and memories weigh a lot and can't always be unloaded in one trip down Memory Lane. I understood she needed to regain her composure as she thought back to how he sounded, the words he used, and what he did that afternoon. I, too, still have those moments.

After a brief moment of tears, Karen returned to looking right in the camera with seriousness and purpose.

"He said I would never get disciplined if he could touch me, and I said, 'No, I can get spanked just like the other kids.'"

Paul continued pushing her by saying, "No. I'll give you a horse."

Karen explained that Paul knew this would be important to her because one of his horses had given birth to a colt she named Cocoa. He offered it to her and gave her $10, which was a significant amount of money at that time, especially to a child.

"Then he said, 'I'll be really gentle, but I'm going to pull your pants down, and I'm going to lick you.'"

Not knowing what else to say to change the conversation or what his words really meant, Karen quietly replied, "Okay." As an innocent 10-year-old with no sexual experience, she did not fully understand what was happening when Paul pulled down her pants and said, "I'm going to lick you."

"At that point, I think I just became numb and just let it happen," she said. "Then he asked when he was done, 'Didn't that feel good?' and I said, 'No,' and he said, 'Well, you're going to think about this, and any time you want to feel good or I want to feel good, you come to me, or I'll come to you, and I'll give you money. You get the colt.'"

Paul followed up his promises of fun things and making each other feel good – far from the discipline discussion for which he supposedly brought her into the room – with intimidation.

"Then he proceeded to tell me that if I told my mom…that the training post, which was a big telephone pole with a whip hanging from it that he used to train the horses, that I would be tied up to it and beat to death," she said, "and he would tell my mom that I was a liar and make sure that she believed it and that when she went to work, I would be killed."

To further help keep Karen quiet about the assault, he told her she could use all the wood, nails, and wheels she wanted. Karen was a bit of a tomboy and had been asking to make a go-kart with Paul's sons. Paul told her that, as the oldest of the kids, she could control the materials and oversee the project with the younger kids.

After Paul let her leave the bedroom, Karen needed to distract her mind from what had taken place. Remembering what he said about the building materials, she went looking for the boys.

"I said, 'Let's make a go-kart. Your dad gave me permission to use as much as I want because I'm the oldest.' When he came out, I wasn't around the wood and nails, so he beat the crap out of his two boys – black and blue eyes, broken noses. That was my go-kart. He shouldn't be hitting them. He beat them up anyway," Karen said.

Just because Paul found the boys with the building materials without his permission, he beat them to the point of nearly requiring hospitalization. Karen fled the area before Paul discovered she was nearby, unsure if the same would happen to her for leaving them unattended.

Trying to get away from the chaos of the ranch and all that happened that day, she rode her bike nearly three miles to a store where she could spend the $10 with which Paul had bribed her. Scared and unsure of whether she should go home or keep riding, she spent the money on a large bag of candy and decided to go home and face whatever was there. She knew if she ran away, he would find her and bring her back, presumably to kill her if she tried to run again.

Karen said, "I went out to the bushes and hid until my mom got home because I didn't know what to do. When she got home, she saw his boys beat up, and I heard her screaming, 'What did you do to your boys? What happened to the boys?' He said, 'I don't know what you're talking about.' She said, 'They're beat up. What did you do?' He told her that they had used the nails and the wood and that he didn't give them permission to, and she asked him where I was."

Karen was still hiding in the bushes watching the scene unfold, too scared to come out of hiding. She was far enough away to feel safe but close enough to hear her mother yelling.

"She kept screaming, 'Where's Karen?! Where's Karen?!' Paul didn't look for me or anything. I finally came out right before dark. She asked me what was wrong, and I said, 'I can't tell you.' She said, 'Yes, you can.'"

"I said, 'No, I can't tell you.' What was going through her mind seeing her daughter hiding and her boyfriend's kids beat up? I don't know what she was thinking, but I would not tell her what happened until he finally said, 'Go ahead. Tell your mom whatever you think happened. Make her shut up because she thinks something happened that didn't happen.'"

Karen looked at Paul and her mother, and the truth began spilling out as she said, "'No, I'm not going to tell my mom because you said you'd kill me if I did,' and he said, 'Okay, well, you're a liar. Tell her what I did.' And I told her."

Karen's mother walked out of the room with Paul, and Karen thought, "Oh, my God, if she doesn't believe me…"

Her mother returned and asked, "Are you *sure* you're telling me the truth?"

Karen said she looked at her mother and very directly said, "If you don't believe me, I'll be dead tomorrow, and then you'll know if I'm telling the truth or not."

When her mother came back one more time from talking privately to Paul, she told Karen, "Start packing your stuff. The police are on their way."

Paul left the ranch, but the police never arrested him that night, even though, according to Karen, they knew where he was. She and Paul's sons were taken to the hospital and examined. After the assault, she never saw Paul's children again, and she and her mother and sisters "kind of went into hiding."

Not long after that, the case went to court. Paul was able to pass a lie detector test, which, at that time, was still admissible in that jurisdiction. He was declared innocent, and all charges were dropped.

Three years passed before Karen received counseling for what happened. By then, she didn't want to revisit the details again for someone new. Her mother had moved the family away from the small town of less than 400 residents where Paul's ranch was to a hectic city of more than 400,000.

"This had been three years I'd had to deal with it. No counseling. I was mad because I was like, 'I haven't even thought about it anymore, Mom. Why do I have to go to counseling?' but she made me go. Mom wrote down a map of the city bus route and gave me money to get on the bus and where to go and made me figure it out on my own. She drove me there the first time, and after that, I had to go on my own. It was six months maybe. The first day that I took the bus, I remember waiting and a drunk guy almost getting hit on the street. She didn't like to drive me anywhere really."

I sensed the statement that Karen hadn't "even thought about it anymore" was not as accurate as she would have liked it to be. In fact, I got the distinct impression she had thought about Paul's abuse of authority, his assault on her innocence, and the horrible way she was introduced to sex many times in the 40 years that had passed.

I asked if she had shared her story with the important people in her life, such as her husband or her children. Something that impacted her to such a degree would seem to be something her loved ones should know. Some survivors have said they find it difficult to share their experiences with a significant other for a variety of reasons ranging from fear of how they'll react, to shame, to simply not wanting to talk about it after years of trying to move on.

Karen said her husband of 14 years knows and that her "ex-husband knew, but he didn't really care." She has not, however, spoken in detail about the assault with her children.

"I didn't go into all the details," she said. "All three of my boys seem to take after their dad. He didn't ever hit me but was very verbally and mentally abusive. I get that from my kids, too. If I don't give them money because I know that they've squandered their money away or are not doing what they should – I'm all about supporting when you need help, but if you're not trying to do something good, I don't help. So, when I don't give them money, the words come out just like their father. I guess I'm too afraid to tell them what happened in detail because I have a feeling they'd come back and be like, 'You deserved it' in one of their outbursts. I'm pretty much an open book with my kids, but that one I'm just…"

Yes, Karen is strong. She weathered storms that might have been more than a weaker person could endure – sexual assault at 10 years old, not knowing anything about her biological father except his name until finding him as an adult, moving more times than she could count before she was a teenager, hearing her mother say she would give up her children for boyfriends, growing up in a home where she was constantly told, "I can't wait until you're 18 so I can kick you out of the house." Despite her outward strength, a current of turmoil that began with a life of instability lies just beneath the surface.

I asked if thoughts of what happened cause problems for her now. She said as much as she tries not to let them, she can't help that there are times when she still feels overwhelmed.

"Like, if somebody is sucking on a sucker, and you hear that sucking sound," she said, making a slurping sound and motion as if she had a lollipop in her mouth, with a sad, pained expression. "I cannot stand that because that's the sound I heard at 10 years old."

Referring to how her relationships have evolved as an adult, she said, "There are some intimacy issues, but I've learned through counseling that on good days, I can go, 'This is not my betrayer. This is my husband.' But there's other days, I'm just like, 'Just stop. I can't do this.'"

Her mother has been sober since Karen was 13, and Karen said she is proud of her for that success. However, Karen said she and her mother rarely got along when she was younger and still don't.

"She's very narcissistic, but for one of the few times in my life, she actually believed me (about the assault). There were many of her boyfriends she said she'd give her children up for if we got in the way."

Karen still struggles with understanding her mother and how to communicate with her after a lifetime of difficulties.

"I know you have to work on yourself when you quit drinking, but when you have children, you need to work with them, too, and her idea was to throw us in Al-Anon and let us deal with our issues there and not with her," she said. "I had made the comment to her that when I grew up, I would not be married nine times like her and that I would know the father of all my children. Well, I'm on marriage three. The first would be annulment, but our state doesn't honor it, and I do know the father of all my children. Not that it's a slap in the face back at her. I just must've realized it when I was younger. Something's not right, and I don't want to be like my mom."

Karen said she took the things she did appreciate about her mother and instilled that into her relationships with her own children. Where she felt her mother had abandoned her and left her to raise herself, she tried to fill in those gaps for her sons.

"We sat down and ate meals together as a family. We did things together," Karen said. "We'd pack a lunch and go to the park or do a road trip, or when my kids had games and plays and choir and all, I went to their stuff. My mom? I can count on one hand the times she came to see my stuff."

Karen and her mother didn't speak for five years until Karen decided to find her biological father. Karen reached out to her mother and made amends in an effort to preserve what little relationship was left despite feeling she had done nothing wrong.

After a brief period of surface-level communication and attempts to have some semblance of mother-daughter bond, Karen shared a story with her mother about having a minor disagreement with her husband and "getting in a little tiff like old people. I was laughing about it because it was so stupid to fight like old people in a store, and she came back and told me that I'm a bully, that I treat my husband like a slave, and that all I care about is money."

Hurt once again by her mother's cruelty, Karen withdrew into her own life, studied a self-help book about toxic and narcissistic mothers, and worked on healing from the pains of the past. After focused efforts to center herself and to find forgiveness for her mother's words and for the hurtful years that had compounded to that point, Karen emailed her mother to say, "I'm ready to communicate again, but I have my own boundaries I want to set, and one is you cannot personally attack me anymore. You can't put me down, and you can't make me feel bad about myself."

Her mother never responded. Karen's standing up for herself and drawing clear boundaries around what she was willing to accept and not accept were not well received. Karen moved on.

"I've accepted we're never going to have the mother-daughter relationship where I can go to her with anything but happy stuff. I told her life isn't always happy, and I wish you could be the mom that I could go to like my other friends' parents, and I said, 'In a good mother-daughter relationship, I should be able to go to you with anything,' and she said, 'I don't know where you think that's a good relationship.'"

Karen talks to a former foster mother with whom she remained in close contact throughout the years and said that woman is "kind of like a second mom." Since finding her biological father, she is getting to know not only that side of her family but that side of herself as well and has a stepmother who, while not much older than Karen herself, is someone she gets along with quite well.

Karen is many years into a lifetime forever changed by a sexual predator named Paul and a mother who left her to raise herself. Yes, Karen *is* strong, but beneath the exterior of a woman who has seen much, known much, done much, and survived much is a 10-year-old girl hiding in the bushes who really just wanted a family and someone to protect her.

She is healed, but the cracks will always be there.

Chapter Eighteen

Blossom

One of the toughest decisions while writing this book was which survivor's story to place at the end. From the beginning, I knew it would be important to choose a final story with the right impact, but what was that? What did that look, feel, and sound like?

Each time I interviewed someone new, the time I spent with each person was something I had to step away from for a few days before writing. Sharing such private information with someone is difficult at best. It's intimate, personal, painful. There were tears and hugs. There were moments of silence in which time seemingly stood still. I sat patiently as survivors – grandmothers, mothers, daughters, sisters, aunts, friends, stay-at-home mothers, business professionals, young women, older women, each one – strained to quiet their brain's deafening rage as their mouths tried to tell stories through filtered hearts still consumed with pains that will never go away.

And so, my interviews brought me to Blossom, the final survivor who is, without a shadow of a doubt, as are all the survivors detailed here, more than what happened to her. What a beautiful name Blossom is. Each person interviewed picked her own pseudonym, which was randomly chosen to avoid recognizable ties to the people discussed, but this one – oh this one! – I cannot think of a better name for a person.

Blossom has one of the most contagious smiles of anyone you'll ever meet. She brings light to any room she enters, and immediately people glow and grow. In whatever situation she is planted, she adapts. She encourages others to do the same, and she is a go-to person for problem-solving and creativity. Blossom is a people person, and anyone around her for more than a minute will get to know her. Her personal life is not as rosy as her personality, though. Underneath the wholehearted laugh is a heart with holes that will never be filled.

"I have told this story twice," Blossom said, as we sat down to begin our interview late on a hot summer afternoon. "One being where I addressed it on Facebook and then (to) my sister."

After years of holding onto her pain, Blossom took to Facebook in the early days of the social media platform to find Everett, the man who assaulted her 35 years ago.

"I honestly hate that guy," she said, "and I remember when Facebook first came out, I said, 'I've got to find him and tell him what he did to me all those years ago.'"

I asked if she found him, hoping she had a chance to confront the man who assaulted her.

"No, I couldn't find him, and I'm hoping he's dead, you know, because I hated him so much. I was so innocent and playful."

The assault took place at Blossom's church while she and her sister were attending youth group activities, as they did every Sunday.

Blossom said, "We were at church. We were youth. We had a youth meeting, choir rehearsal on a Saturday. Normally at the church, we would have one adult, a youth leader or youth director or choir director, and they would leave. One person would stay behind to lock the doors, and so we were getting ready to close everything out. I would always go into either the secretary's room or the pastor's study, and I would be the one to go and call my mom to come and pick us up because we were young. We couldn't drive.

"I left the choir stand, and I went to the back to make that phone call. There was a little closed-in room, and I closed the door and called my mom. When I turned around, there was this guy who was also in the church."

The guy was Everett. Blossom had seen him there on Saturdays when the youth met, but he wasn't a regular church member. He was a couple of years older than she was, and she recognized him as someone who went to school with her sister.

"He came in, too, and I didn't think anything of it," Blossom said, "so I called my mom and told her that we were getting ready to close out and that she could come to pick us up. I hung up the phone. I moved over to the side to let him by, and he moved over with me. I was like, 'Okay...' At that point, he attacked me. He started groping me and touching all over me, and I remember fighting back. I was thinking, 'This is *not good*!' Then, I scratched him. I remember scratching him."

Blossom's voice cracked as she described the assault, and I could tell some of the smaller details like where he stood, how he moved, the way she scratched him were things she hadn't allowed herself to think about in detail for many years. The tears started to flow. Her words became urgent as she spoke, as if she were once again that little girl trapped in the small room with a second chance to get out and a desire to scratch harder, move faster, and rewrite history.

"I got out of there," she continued, "and by that time, everybody was in the front of the church. We were just kind of closing out, so they were holding hands to do an altar prayer, and he came out of that room and came right up there to the altar prayer, and he stood right beside me and held my hand like he hadn't…done…a single… thing. And I remember him while he was holding my hand, he was rubbing, like rubbing his hands against my hands, and I wanted to *scream*."

Whether consciously or subconsciously, Blossom was furiously rubbing her own hands while she told me how Everett held her hand during the altar prayer. She went from rubbing her hand as he had done to rubbing it as if she were trying to make it clean again, and her tears were flowing more and more as if she were in the moment once again and I wasn't in the room.

"And so. Geez. I was young, so that hurt. That bothered me psychologically. I told my sister."

Upon mentioning her sister, we had to take a break while I found a box of tissues. She continuously apologized. I reassured her that she had nothing for which to apologize. What she was feeling was real, necessary, and long overdue, but so many survivors offer that same apology.

I'm sorry for grief.
I'm sorry for inconveniencing you.
I'm sorry to share my truths.
I'm sorry for taking your time.
I'm sorry for burdening you with this knowledge.
I'm sorry for the fact that this happened.

I don't believe Blossom feels in any way that what happened was her fault. She is not a delicate flower in need of saving. From our discussion, it was clear she knows where the blame should be placed. She isn't a survivor who ever spent a second wondering if she led on her attacker or if she had some part in what took place. However, she *is* someone still harboring unprocessed grief and shouldering unshared truths, both of which have more than taken their toll over the years.

"I remember telling my sister because she was always the protective one, and I told her what happened," she said. "I remember her confronting him, but it didn't go any further than that. She went to confront him, and by that time, my mother had come to pick us up, and I remember seeing him. He was walking down by the church. I remember my sister saying something about she was going to get him."

Blossom's sister never had a chance to catch up with Everett. They never saw him at church again, and Blossom never attended regularly after that day. She lost the desire to be involved for fear she might see him.

"At that point, I would tell my sister, 'I don't want to go back to church. I don't want to do anything with the youth. I don't want to be in choir anymore.' There were times my sister would go to church, and I just wouldn't go because I didn't want to see him again. I remember him after church walking down the sidewalk by the church just like it was nothing."

She sighed and wiped the tears from her eyes. I looked across the table and said simply, "It *wasn't* anything to *him*. That's the problem."

"I'm sorry," Blossom said, again apologizing for her tears.

"Don't be sorry," I said. "It's how you feel, and it's real."

Something about saying how she felt really lit a fire in her as grief and tears turned to a mild case of rage.

"And it probably wasn't the first time that he had done that," she exclaimed, "but I did absolutely nothing to lead him on! I mean, I was a youngster! I hated him so much, and I never saw him again, but I hated him. I hated him. I hated him! And probably to this day, I probably still hate him because he doesn't know what he did to me, you know? To touch all over me, and I was a virgin. I was young. But to catch me off-guard and to feel over me and violate me and then to come while we're doing altar prayer and hold my hand and just rub it and you know I was just shaking…I just hate that guy."

As her pain poured out about Everett, Blossom continued talking about how she felt that day and how she talked to her sister, how she hoped her sister would catch up with Everett, and how she never rid herself of the torment of what happened. When I asked Blossom to be interviewed, I knew this was the story she planned to tell; however, in the course of our interview, another incident worked its way into the conversation, a story I don't think she intended to share but one I feel is important to understanding her, to understanding the unexpected dangers of sexual predators, and to understanding that not every incident is a physical attack.

"I remember I was a freshman in high school and in my neighborhood, we used to have a store that was maybe three blocks from us. It was a safe neighborhood back then. I remember going to the store. This guy had this brown Mustang, and he kept following me. He was driving really slowly, and I'm just walking by myself because we had walked that way before.

"I got to the store, and he pulls up at the store and gets on the pay phone. That's just how long ago this was. He got on the pay phone, and I went in the store, got what I needed, and walked out. When I walk out, I notice he hangs up the pay phone, gets in his car, and drives off."

As Blossom got closer to home, she was walking off the sidewalk near the curb along the roadside as the man in the brown Mustang pulled up not far away.

"He says, 'Excuse me,' and I looked up, and I said, 'Yes?' He said, 'Can you tell me where Dick Taylor is?' and automatically in my head I'm saying, 'Oh yeah, he's lost,' so I said, 'Well, if you go up to this street and turn…' and while I'm talking and walking, his car is moving closer and closer to me. I look in and he is masturbating. I screamed. I ran and got on the sidewalk, and I was shaking. I was like, 'Why did he do this?!'"

Blossom hurried straight home and told her sister and her sister's best friend what happened. Being the responsible older sister who had already gone through the incident with Everett with her and seen the effects, Blossom's sister told her, "We've got to tell."

Blossom said, "I told my mom and dad, and I love my mom and dad, but they asked me why I was walking to the store. That was something I did all the time. We would always walk to the store. I didn't walk to the store anymore after that. That was it for me. But I know my sister and her friend were highly upset and told her friend's brothers, who were like, 'Who is he?!?'"

Just as with Everett, though, nothing happened. Blossom said she didn't know the man, although she did see him one more time while she was on the bus coming home from school one day, and she pointed him out to her sister yelling, "That's the guy!" She was always looking for him after that, and getting the image of what he did out of her memory hasn't been easy to forget, even after all these years.

"I remember I looked inside, and he had his penis out, and he's just going at it. You would think an incident that tiny would get out of your head, but no. That affected me," she said.

I asked whether Everett's assault on her at the church had caused ongoing effects in her relationships as she developed into a teenager or now as an adult.

"You know what? It affected me in relationships because I don't like anyone touching me," she replied very matter-of-factly. "I don't want anybody touching my breasts. I don't want anybody touching anything private on me, and I think I have really no strong desire to be sexually active. I can go years (without sexual activity), and it doesn't bother me because I think that did something to me."

"Do you think your lack of sexual desire started that day in the church when Everett assaulted you?" I asked.

"I'm sure it did," Blossom said. "You know, for me to practice abstinence, I don't even think about it, and relationship-wise, I've had several relationships, but with some of them, nothing physically has transpired, so, of course, they end. I couldn't really tell why I wasn't attracted or didn't want to do anything with the guy. I just didn't have a desire. Maybe at that point in my life right then when he did that, any type of sexual desires I had went out the window because of what he did to me. He violated me. He touched me in places that should not have been touched by a complete stranger."

"It seems like he made you feel as if that sort of touching was repulsive. Look at the reaction it's provoking from you all these years later just from talking about it," I said. "That's not okay. That was his fault. Not yours."

Blossom agreed, of course, but I could see on her face, that she could practically still feel Everett's hands shoving her around that small room, groping her, and taking away a power she would never get back. I asked how she felt that day when she got in the car after he assaulted her.

"I was crying. I got in that corner, and I was just quiet," she said.

I asked if her mother had sensed something was wrong or asked why she was so quiet, and she said, "No, she didn't ask anything. My sister was always the talker and the singer, believe it or not. I just liked being there. Every day, I was hoping my sister would come home and tell me she got him. My sister was always the protective one. She was always the one who would go after those people who hurt me. Even now, at this age, if something happens to me, I go to my sister and say, "'Hey, such and such happened' and she's immediately, '*Who is it*?!?'"

Blossom never told anyone the details of the assault except her sister until the day of our interview, a choice she now regrets.

"I didn't tell my pastor who died. I didn't tell his wife. I know my mom and dad would've gone to the police. I know they would have because *that* in a *church*? That was just too much and for him to touch me and violate me? I couldn't move. He was all over me. That was the worst feeling in the world to have somebody touch you that you don't want to have touching you."

"Now that we've talked, will you ever tell anyone else? Will you tell your son or grandchildren?" I asked. "How has this incident affected how you raised your son and how you talk to your grand-children about the type of people you want them to be?"

"I tell my son and my grandchildren, 'You watch how you treat women because those are somebody's children. That woman is somebody's child, somebody's mother. You keep that in mind. It could be me,'" she said. "And I tell my son all the time, 'You know how I know those things? Because I'm a woman, so before you mistreat a woman or do anything like that, think about me.' And so, he has never done that, and I thank God for that. I really do. He has never been abusive. He would punch a hole in a wall before he would hit a woman. If a woman says 'No,' my son is so easygoing. He's like, 'Okay, bye.' He doesn't deal with it. So that's my least concern. I know if I were to die today, my son and my grandchildren would be good. I wouldn't have to worry about them going to jail for something like assault, rape, or abuse, no domestic disputes, and they've never seen it either."

I asked, "Will you ever tell your son what we've talked about today?"

"I can't. I cannot tell him something like that. He's protective, too. My brothers, I couldn't tell them either, especially the one who lives here because he would be all in an uproar, even after all these years, like, 'I know a lot of people. I'm going to find him!' I can't tell *anybody*."

Throughout the process of interviewing survivors, I encountered a variety of perspectives on living with the truth of what happened. For some, the reality is relatively fresh. The sounds, the feelings, the smells, the pain are raw and still being processed. For others, the memories have had generations to process and still feel as if they happened a minute ago. Some have opened up to friends and family about their assaults and tried to work through it. For others, being interviewed was an opportunity to open up for the first time to loved ones and begin a new phase of healing.

For Blossom, the pain of her assault has lingered just below the surface for most of her life, and even now, she is trapped in the feeling that she "can't tell anybody." Like many survivors who look back and wish they had told someone when it happened, she lives with the regret of not coming forward and holding her assaulter accountable. He got to walk away, and she has, in some ways, been frozen in that moment since that day.

Blossom is successful. She has raised a loving family. She is the light of her friends' circle. She is creative and smart, kind and generous. She enjoys gardening, cooking, crafting, spending time with friends and family and is definitely the person you can count on if you want to do something spontaneously fun. By outward impressions, you would never suspect the turmoil and pain she hides.

Blossom was the ideal choice for the final survivor's story. While most of the survivors I interviewed had stories that tended toward finding a loving spouse who renewed their faith in good people or dealing with the pain of what happened, reconciling their feelings, and moving on with life, Blossom's story is not the same. After all these years, she still deals with confusion and grief as if Everett just stepped up next to her in that prayer circle and she still feels the clamminess of his arrogance rubbing her hand. Even if she doesn't think about him every hour or every day like some survivors whose assaults happened more recently, her trauma feels as if it just happened. If she were to pass that church, she would, no doubt, look for him on the sidewalk.

So, Blossom was my choice for ending this book as the final story. As I interviewed survivors, they related how they dealt with what happened, found love, turned to God, prayed, or found solace in certain things. They found some sort of strength to move on and set their assaulter aside in their lives. Blossom, while a healthy, well-adjusted, happy, successful, dynamic woman, is not the same. Her pain is unresolved. She is a reminder that no matter how much time passes, survivors who aren't able to deal with their trauma and are left feeling they have no one to talk to can continue to live with tears and pain right below the surface.

I wondered if, after all these years, Blossom thought she would do anything differently that day.

"You said you came up swinging and scratching at him. If you had it to do over again, what would you do differently?" I asked. "Do you think it would've made a difference?"

"I probably would've picked up the phone and knocked the heck out of him, but he caught me off-guard," she replied.

"If you, as the person you are now, could impart wisdom to the person you were then," I asked, "what would you say to that girl in that moment?"

"Kick, scream, and let everybody know before he got out of that church," Blossom said, without hesitation. "That was not a secret that should have been kept. I should have made a *big* deal out of it, and he should never have gotten out of that church. *Never.* He should not have been able to hold my hand in that prayer circle. He should not have been able to walk down that sidewalk after church. He should not have been. And I don't care how old or how young he was, I was young, too, and he violated me. Don't make excuses for somebody else's actions. Hold them accountable. Don't push it under the rug. *Don't sweep it under the rug.* Don't walk away from it. If you're violated, that's personal. *Fight for yourself.* You *have* to be your own advocate. *You have to.*"

I can't think of anyone who is a better advocate for the things she believes in than Blossom. She is passionate about life, about her family, about her beliefs. To know her is to love her, but don't be mistaken by her seemingly easygoing nature – she doesn't tolerate rude behavior in any age and will put you in your place and make you like it (a skill many good Southern women have, but Blossom has it down to a science).

Perhaps part of her ability to draw people in and make them comfortable around her grew out of the feeling that she wanted to make sure no one ever felt as marginalized as she had felt multiple times at an early age. Perhaps she is a kind soul who understands all people deserve to be treated decently in life. Or perhaps it's a combination of all of the above. Either way, Blossom deserved better than the hand she was dealt, but no one would ever know from the outside looking in. She spends her life making sure everyone around her has the best shot at life they can have, and that, in turn, makes her happy.

We all deal with what happened to us in our own ways. This is Blossom's. She does not want to be in a physical relationship. After 35 years, she still cringes at the thought of being touched intimately. Everett stole that from her. She feels as if she has no one to talk to about it, even after all this time, but I'm so grateful she chose to share her story here so others can hear what she went through and understand how important it is to come forward.

Thirty-five years is a long time to feel alone. Sadly, when Blossom's assault happened, the world was a different place. She was more likely to have been asked, "Why were you in there with him?" "Did you lead him on?" "Why didn't you yell?" "Why didn't you (fill in the blank with any number of things, such as run, punch, etc.)?" or "Why did you wear that dress today?" I would like to think if she came forward today, she would be taken more seriously, but, back then, the reaction would more likely have been "shame" on her family that this took place in the church.

How many Blossoms are in the world? How many people have suffered in silence for years thinking they couldn't talk to anyone? How many Blossoms have to grieve before we realize these are not incidents to be kept in the shadows and shoved into the closet of family secrets?

There is no shame for Blossom. *The shame is Everett's.*

Read that again.

The. Shame. Is. Everett's.

But he walked away. He strolled down the sidewalk and out of Blossom's life. The man in the brown Mustang drove away, zipped up his pants, and considered his job done. He probably showed himself to someone else another day, and the day he preyed on Blossom was most likely not his first encounter.

If there is one Blossom reading this book, I pray she (or he) finds someone to talk to before the pain eats them from the inside out. If there is an Ashley, Brandi, Casey, Elisa, Jessica, Karen, Lola, or any man hiding these secrets, I pray they find someone to talk to whom they can trust.

If you are an assaulter and have made it all the way through this book, I pray for you, too. For every Everett and every man in the Mustang, a prayer goes out.

If you assaulted someone
and understand you did wrong,
ask God for forgiveness.
You have a soul worth saving.
We all do.
If you have been blessed with children,
teach them to do better.
Look within yourself to find out why you did what you did.
Do better, and put only good things into the world.

Thank you for sharing your story, your life, and your light, Blossom. Everett may have walked away, but you have walked into so many lives in positive ways. For every moment of your life he stole, you have granted so much of yourself to others. You are loved. You are worthwhile. You are special. Thank you for reminding us that not every story is tied up nicely with reconciliation and progress but that life does go on. You are a shining example of choosing happiness despite the pain, and I'm so grateful you allowed me to tell your story.

You are more than what happened to you, even if you don't always feel like it.

""...and he came out of that room and came right up there to the altar prayer, and he stood right beside me and held my hand like he hadn't…done…a single…thing. And I remember him while he was holding my hand, he was rubbing, like rubbing his hands against my hands, and I wanted to scream.."

CHAPTER NINETEEN

Living as More

Dear God,

Thank you for this journey.

Thank you for never giving up on me when I gave up on myself and for always trying to tell me something, even when I refused to listen.

Thank you for trusting me to share the stories of these brave people who were willing to find their voice and to bare the ugliness and evil that made them victims alongside the strength and triumphs that make them survivors.

Thank you for the people who love and support us and make us feel worthwhile, and thank you for You.

Because we get to see another day, we each have another chance to tell the world, "I am more than what happened to me," even if sometimes we are the ones who need to hear it.

Thank you for deep breaths, moments of clarity, closed-eye and open-heart reflections, and the healing power of prayer.

When all else feels like it fails in the world of a victim, You are there to help us survive.

In an ideal world, there would be no victims, but the world is not an ideal place. In this less-than-kind world in which we find ourselves, we must unfortunately help victims find the strength and support to become survivors, to march into their futures shame-free and comfortable in the knowledge that they are whole, unbroken, and untarnished.

Sadly, for every person like me, Ashley, Blossom, Brandi, Casey, Elisa, Jessica, Karen, and Lola, there are thousands more, people with their own stories of sexual assault who experienced the pain and loss of personal worth and dignity.

Some have never found someone with whom they feel safe enough to share their story.

Some will take their pain to the grave out of embarrassment.

Some tried to tell someone – maybe *anyone* who would listen – what happened but were shamed into thinking they were at fault.

Some were told what happened wasn't assault because they shouldn't have been in that place or worn those clothes, they knew the person who assaulted them or allowed the person into their home, or because they had been drinking and let their guard down.

Whatever the reason, there are many people who will never tell their stories. They will silently suffer for the remainder of their lives, dealing daily with things that repeatedly remind them of the pain, shame, and perhaps even fear.

Life after sexual assault does not have to be lived that way, but no one other than the survivor can make that choice, can be ready for the painful reality that can follow emerging from the sexual assault shadows and stepping with some level of confidence into the harsh light of acceptance. If that's you, if you're spending more time unsure of how to embrace a stronger future, only you can take the first step from victim to survivor.

At some point in life, your choice was stolen. *Only you* get to decide when the time arrives to exhale the past and breathe in a life of more. *Only you* get to reclaim your voice when the time is right and say with whatever confidence you can find the first time you say it,

> *I am more than what happened to me.*
> *I choose more. I choose me.*
> *I choose to believe I am more –*
> *today and tomorrow and every day.*

If you are trying to support a survivor, you can't force the moment of personal acceptance, no matter how much you would like to and no matter how much you think it will help. All you can do is continue to be reassuring and allow the person the freedom to come forward when they are ready.

The best thing you can say is, "You are more than what happened to you. I'm here ready to help and to listen whenever you're ready to feel like more. Until then, take the time you need to heal. I can't try to be *more*, but I can try to be *enough* for both of us for now."

I trudged through nearly 20 years of feeling like less before I was ready to live as more. Regardless of the persistent feeling that God was "trying to tell me something" and that I was supposed to use my story as a platform for others' voices, I'd settled deep into the shadows of shame refusing to acknowledge what took place.

Because of that, I spent many years allowing negativity into my life and seeking it to a high degree out of a feeling that it was what I deserved. Even after deciding I would no longer allow the past's shadows to creep into my life's light and that I would let my voice be heard, it still took several years to write this book.

I started. I wrote. I set writing timelines and goals.

I stopped. I couldn't do it. I recoiled at the idea of revealing to my family and friends what I planned to publish.

I wrote again with a renewed strength and determination.

I put it away and spent months using lack of people to interview and no time to work on it as excuses. I used any ridiculous reasoning to push myself away.

Finally, I wrote. And then I wrote some more.

And I didn't accept my attempts at justifications for the delays as anything other than excuses to keep me out of some sort of perceived trouble I was getting myself into by revealing so many deeply personal details.

But for years the weight of what I was working on, the memories I had to revisit, and the knowledge that I had to discuss it with the people I loved the most sat on my chest like that Mr. Bear who swallowed the lead pipe filled with concrete. You know the one – that burdensome boy bound in 100 yards of razor blades and barbed wire dipped in a blistering cocktail of rubbing alcohol and hot sauce – yeah, that guy.

He certainly couldn't forget his favorite blanket to smother me in, stitched with those threads of panic attack, shame, and embarrassment either. Of course not. Writing this book couldn't possibly be accomplished without his relentless presence.

By the time I was halfway through my own story and arranging interviews with survivors, I had nearly smothered myself under the weight of it all by allowing the "Mr. Bear" of negativity and feeling like less to consume me. I had to talk to my husband about things I swore no other living soul would ever know, and I waited until I was almost completely finished writing to talk to my parents and in-laws. I actually avoided spending too much time with my parents for the better part of two years out of a ridiculously immature desire to avoid the topic.

It was my story to tell, and I finally wrote it. I hope I gave the survivors I was honored to work with a chance to feel their voices were heard, and I pray there are survivors reading this who identify with what they read and find themselves wanting to live as more. If there are supporters reading this, I hope they understand that the fact they know our stories and are trusted to share our journey to more is significant.

I pray my daughters will never know what it means to be a sexual assault survivor more than having read these stories and that they will live in a world where people understand better how to treat each other with respect, dignity, and kindness. If they or someone they know ever finds themselves in a situation where they are being assaulted, I hope they know how to react, how to report what happened, and that there is no shame in what took place.

As for me, I will continue living each day refusing to allow the people who hurt me to steal another second of my life.

I am more than what happened to me.

I AM more.

I.

Am.

MORE.

I am MORE.

Yes, I AM.

We all are.

We are more than what was done to us.

We are more than how we were treated.

We are more than what was said to us and about us.

We are more than what we thought about ourselves.

We are more than how we acted in the days, weeks, months, and years since then.

We are more than what happened.

We. Are. More.

ABOUT THE AUTHOR

Devan Millsong chose a pseudonym because "small towns like to talk with big mouths about things they don't understand, and people deserve a chance to move on." Since moving on from her sexual assault and working through the healing process of putting a broken world back together, Devan spends her blessedly boring life as a mother of three in a rural town in Louisiana with the love of her life who was once the "boy down the street." Devan has received several leadership awards throughout her career, is a freelance writer, and is active in the nonprofit world. She earned a bachelors in journalism, masters in journalism with secondary concentrations in public administration and speech communication, and a masters in education, but she will tell you none of that has anything to do with being smart. It mostly means she doesn't know what she wants to be when she grows up. Since the minute she could pick up a pencil and draw lines on paper, she has written poetry, short stories, journals, speeches, and random ideas. These days, she isn't a little girl scratching lines on paper and calling it a story anymore, but she is no less ready to say, "Look, Mama! Look, Daddy! Look what I wrote."